LEARNING ASTROLOGY

LEARNING ASTROLOGY

AN ASTROLOGY BOOK FOR BEGINNERS

☉ ☽

DAMIAN SHARP

WEISERBOOKS
San Francisco, CA / Newburyport, MA

First published in 2005 by
RED WHEEL/WEISER, LLC
York Beach, ME
With offices at:
500 3rd Street, Suite 230
San Francisco, CA 94107
www.redwheelweiser.com

Library of Congress Cataloging-in-Publication Data

Sharp, Damian.
Learning astrology : an astrology book for beginners / Damian Sharp.
p. cm.
ISBN 1-57863-298-6
1. Astrology. 2. Horoscopes. I. Title.
BF1708.1.S52 2005
133.5—dc22   2005018474

Typeset in Adobe Caslon by Kathryn Sky-Peck
Printed in Canada
FR

12 11 10 09 08 07 06
8 7 6 5 4 3 2

For Yumika, Venus in Furs,
alluring and enigmatic
like moonlight on a placid lake.
—DS

CONTENTS

PART 1

SURVEYING THE HOROSCOPIC SKYSCAPE

CHAPTER 1

THE HOROSCOPE AND THE SIGNS OF THE ZODIAC

Astrology is both a science and an art. It is a symbolic representation of all of the elements—religious, spiritual, emotional, mental, and physical, invisible and visible—that exist in the universe and come together in diverse combinations that account for individual human beings and the forces that shape and act upon them. We are microcosms manifesting the macrocosm, an ancient concept set forth in the Bible as Man made in the image of God. Astrological interpretation relies heavily on an informed intuition and a familiarity, gained from practice and time, with the complex and multilayered meanings underlying its seemingly simple symbology. Interpreting a horoscope is partly science, partly intuitive discipline, and ultimately a synthesis of both. The particular reading will reflect the personality and outlook of the astrologer in much the same way as a psychologist's analysis is also colored by his or her personal views.

Astrology tells us that as individuals we are peculiar and particular, while at the same time a direct manifestation of a cosmic whole to which we are inexorably linked. It reminds us that we are bound to the karmic wheel, that we come into the world with special gifts as well as certain burdens and travails. On the surface it can appear to tell us that our fortunes and our personalities are preordained, that our fates are completely in the hands of the gods. But a man's character is his fate, the Greek philosopher Heracleitus tells us, and in the end there is no disguising or excusing who we are.

Correctly understood and applied, a horoscope is a precise instrument based on real forces, events, and relationships occurring in nature. It is, most importantly, a diagram of an individual's purpose in life and a symbolic language that describes how different factors—signs, planets, and houses—are combined to produce a meaningful whole. Each horoscope is a complex combination of factors, a graphic depiction of a particular determining and synchronistic moment in time and space when the bodies of the solar system form a unique pattern. The art of astrological analysis lies in intuitively synthesizing all the relationships in the horoscope to create a complete and integrated picture or profile.

In reading any horoscope, it is important to remember that the energies symbolized by the planets and signs represent birth potentials that the individual may or may not choose to actualize in the manner described. Age, sex, socioeconomic conditions, education, environment, spiritual development, and many other factors contribute to the ways in which we express our natal energies.

Astrology does not preclude personal willpower, self-determination, and dynamic action upon those very forces that seem to have cosmically preordained who we are and what we are to become. What it presents us with are the lessons we need to learn within this particular turn of the Great Wheel, along with our innate potential, in order to become and ultimately be. How well we learn these lessons and gain from them is up to us as individuals. We are all, in a sense, Odysseus using all of his courage, guile, strength, and wits to defy Poseidon (the god of the sea), of whom he'd made an enemy, in order to simply get home. How well the lessons are learned is not the responsibility of the teacher, who simply presents them for what they are and moves on. It relies solely on the intelligence, receptivity, perception, and tenacity of the pupil.

CONSTRUCTING A HOROSCOPE OR ASTROLOGICAL CHART

You may find it useful to obtain a horoscope for your time and place of birth so you can learn the principles presented in this book by studying your own natal, or birth, chart. Constructing an individual horoscope is a fairly complex process, involving precise calculations, the exact time, date, and place of birth, latitude and longitude, an ephemeris, a table of the houses, a list of time changes, and other tools. In this day and age, however, there are many Internet sites and computer software programs for casting astrological charts. Several books on casting techniques are also available, among them Alan Leo's *Casting the Horoscope* and Margaret Hone's *Modern Textbook of*

Astrology. The American Federation of Astrologers (AFA) also puts out an excellent series of math handbooks.

THE ORIGINS OF ASTROLOGY

In our earliest art, that of the Upper Paleolithic, between 32,000 to 12,000 years ago, depictions of the heavens, of the Sun, Moon, and the stars, are totally absent. Our remote Cro-Magnon ancestors were not stargazers beyond an awareness of the moon and its phases, depicted, perhaps, in bas-relief cave carvings of women holding bison horns with thirteen incisions and as marks on antlers and bones found on the cave floors. These people were basically earthbound in their preoccupations, concerned with their immediate and animistic world. For them, magic and power resided not in the sky above, but in the earth, in deep caves in which these ancient artists chose to render, by the meager light of crude lamps and small fires, remarkably beautiful, sophisticated, and accurately detailed depictions of the fauna that both sustained and threatened their existence: aurochs, bison, horses, ibex, and reindeer; mammoth, rhino, lion, and the cave-dwelling bear. The symbolic meaning beyond their naturalistic representations spoke of the creatures' inherent personalities and attributes, as well as a host of abstract ideas associated with them (like speed, agility, courage, strength, nurturing, fierceness, cunning). Chinese astrology is in part based on this kind of observation. What did these creatures represent to our ancestors, who knew and observed them so intimately? It does seem that the images on the cave walls are not just the beginning of art, but the beginnings of written language, visual symbols drawn from nature conveying meanings beyond their simple mundane representations.

The deep cave is the realm of the shaman, of the vision quest, of the underworld where nature's mysterious power, the miracle of existence itself—birth, being, death, and regeneration—reside. It was the role of the shaman-artist to penetrate this dark realm of the invisible and make contact with and capture this power, conjuring the animals and their attributes from out of the living rock in which their spirit-essence dwelled and snaring them as though art was the hunter's trap. The creation of these magnificent works of art was usually part of a form of ritualistic magic.

With the end of the last Ice Age, hunter-gatherer cultures were gradually replaced by nomadic tent-dwelling herders with their domesticated flocks and agrarian and city-building societies as civilization began its long emergence. Having solved certain earthbound problems and reduced mundane concerns, the philosophically minded began to look upward to observe and ponder the glowing bodies in the firmament and their cyclic movements across the sky, which observers came to correlate with the changes of the seasons and other earthly events. In observing how the seasons of the year and the movement of the stars and planets followed fixed and correlating laws of change and transformation, they identified a possible relationship between the earth and the sky and a key to understanding the nature of all beings in time and space. Determining the meaning of the influence of the stars and planets became the role of the astrologer-priests. Thus, astrology came into being as a practice that belonged to the priesthood and the royalty they served.

Almost all ancient peoples from the Mesolithic period onward had some system of reading the heavens for divinatory purposes. The belief and study of celestial omens without the use of a chart, or a map of the stars, do not constitute what we call astrology. The most commonly held belief among scholars is that astrology came into being in Mesopotamia (the region between the Tigris and Euphrates rivers in what is modern Iraq). Around 6000 B.C.E., Babylonians observed the planets as "wanderers," and early Babylonian records attest to the existence of astrology as we know it today, that is, a horoscopic astrology used for predicting the future, answering questions, and analyzing an individual's destiny based on the time and place of birth. Initially, Mesopotamian astrology was much like that of other cultures: a simple reading of the heavens for omens that might effect or foretell happenings on earth. However, the Mesopotamians soon developed a system that identified recurring patterns in the night sky and their direct correspondence to human events. The first known astrological texts, written in cuneiform on clay tablets, are from the old Babylonian period around the time of Hammurabi, the king who introduced the first written rule of law known as the Hammurabi Code and quoted in the Old Testament—"An eye for an eye, a tooth for a tooth." Like the peoples of many other cultures, the Mesopotamians believed that the stars and planets were in fact gods and goddesses. Venus was Ishtar, one of their major deities. The Egyptians identified the constellation Orion with Osiris, the god of the underworld. The Mesopotamians however were unique in their view of the stars and planets as being indicators of divine will at any given moment in time, the here and now, thus making them the originators of astrology as we understand it today.

The evolution of astrology seems to have gone through three major phases. First came the development of lore surrounding the observation of omens. Then came the development of a Zodiac, without personal horoscopes, of twelve signs through which the transits of Jupiter were recorded at the rate of one sign per year. From this, some believe, came the basis for the Chinese system of assigning each year to a zodiacal animal sign (the Chinese animal signs have a direct correlation to Western zodiacal signs). Then came horoscopic astrology, involving the casting of personal birth charts.

In the fifth century B.C.E., the Chaldeans developed rules for erecting royal horoscopes. April 29, 409 B.C.E. is the oldest known Babylonian horoscope for an individual. It was also Chaldean astrologers who were the "Three Kings," or Magi, who traveled from Persia to pay homage to the newborn Christ with their symbolic gifts of gold, frankincense, and myrrh—gold for royalty, frankincense for divinity, and myrrh for death (embalming) and healing—meaning that Christ was king, god (in Buddhist terms, a Bodhisattva), and physician. The Magi, or astrologer-priests, held special positions of power in Babylonian society.

The Babylonians became particularly adept, based on the records of their observations, at accurately predicting the positions of the planets at any given time in the future. Systematic eclipse records were kept from 747 B.C.E. into the Hellenistic period.

With the conquest of Persia and Egypt by Alexander the Great, Babylonian ideas, in particular astrology, were incorporated into Persian, Egyptian, and Hellenic cultures. In 331 B.C.E., following Alexander's conquests, Mesopotamian astrology was introduced into Greece. Around 280 B.C.E., Berossus, a Chaldean astrologer and historian, directly related events to star movements and worship.

Greek astrology took a more personal form than that of Mesopotamia, with the assignment of mythological correspondences to the Zodiac and planets. Indeed, natal astrology grew in popularity after the Greeks introduced their humanistic and individualistic ideas into Chaldean star lore. The Stoics appear to have been particularly receptive to it, and the medical ideas of Hippocrates were apparently influenced by it.

Around 280 B.C.E., Rome began to be strongly affected by Greek astrology. In 135 B.C.E., Posidinius furthered astrology among Roman intellectuals. Later, it was opposed by Cicero and the Epicureans. In 70 B.C.E., the Greeks set up the first-known personal horoscope based on the exact time of birth, thus deriving the Ascendant. In 30 B.C.E., the Emperor Augustus had his horoscope erected and interpreted by Thrasyllus, establishing a precedent that was followed by later Roman emperors.

According to some theorists, the birthplace of astrology as we have defined it was pharaonic Egypt. In 1375 B.C.E., the pharaoh Akhenaton established monotheistic sun worship, only to be overthrown by the priesthood and the army, which feared that this monumental change in the established order of Egyptian society made Egypt vulnerable to a Hittite invasion armed with a new weapon, the iron sword. That the Egyptians were accomplished astronomers we have no doubt. The accurate alignment of the pyramids and other temples to certain fixed stars clearly attests to this. But it is a later Egypt, one influenced by Babylonian ideas brought first by the Persians and then by the Greeks, that became the primary source of horoscopic astrology.

The Egyptian texts referred to in later astrological literature were written in Greek. When Alexander the Great conquered the Persian Empire and Egypt and penetrated into northwestern India, Greek became the dominant language from North Africa to the far reaches of Central Asia. Even the Bactrian peoples of what is today Afghanistan and Pakistan had Greek-speaking rulers into the early centuries of the Common Era. Ancient statues of Buddha draped in Greek togas (known as "Hellenic Buddhas") are still relatively common (or were, as many were destroyed as pagan idols by the Taliban in Afghanistan). As a result, the Babylonian beliefs embodied in Egyptian astrology traveled easily to India.

In the West, astrology reached a high point with the Greeks and the Romans. Around 10 C.E., the poet-astrologer Manilius wrote his *Astronomicon*, the first major Greek work on astrology, and astrology was embraced by several of the Mediterranean mystery religions, some of which had come from the East. In 140 C.E., Ptolemy of Alexandria published his *Tetrabiblos*, the first major textbook on astrology. In the fourth century C.E. after Rome's conversion to Christianity, St. Augustine led an early Christian attack on astrology. It experienced a resurrection under the reign of the emperor Constantine after Julius Firmicus Maternus published his *Mathesis* supporting astrological theories and beliefs. The fall of the Roman Empire saw the decline of astrology in the West.

During the Middle Ages, the Arabs kept divinatory astrology alive, and it was reintroduced to medieval Europe by Islamic scholars in the universities of Spain during the Moorish conquests. Around 800 C.E., Charlemagne became fascinated and influenced by the craft and helped further promote it in the West. In the eighth century, a school of astrology was established in Baghdad, and Chinese astrology was developed by Han Yu and Li Hsu-Chung. In the ninth century, Sabian star worship took firm root in Mesopotamia and Albumasar published his *Introduction to Astrology*.

In England during the twelfth century, after journeying to the Middle East, Adelard of Bath was instrumental in reintroducing astrology to the Christian West. Later, St. Thomas Aquinas helped reconcile astrology with the teachings of the Church. Universities in France and Spain then adopted its study and established chairs in its name. During the Renaissance, the astrologer/physician Paracelsus and others furthered its acceptance and development. Astrology became associated with alchemy, magic, and other occult arts. But by the mid-1540s, the Copernican view of the universe was seen as a scientific refutation of geocentric astrology. In 1555, Nostradamus published the first of his "prophecies," and soon after Catherine de' Medici and several other rulers of the period became passionate believers in astrology. The Danish astronomer Tycho Brahe, who was also Johannes Kepler's teacher, secretly practiced astrology, and later Kepler actually sought to develop a new astrology. But all of this activity ultimately did little to stem astrology's fall into disrepute. In 1666, astrology was officially banished as superstition from the French Academy of Sciences.

Astrology's hidden appeal and knowledge, however, remained irresistible, like a forbidden fruit. In the seventeenth century, a Benedictine monk and teacher, Placidus de Titus, published a series of important astrological works, which were widely well received. He was followed by the court astrologer and physician to Louis XIV of France, Morin de Villefranche, whose *Astrologia Gallica* also had a profound and widespread effect. In England, William Lilly published a major literary work on astrology in 1675 and successfully predicted the 1676 fire in London. However, astrology continued to be practiced mainly by charlatans and during the Age of Enlightenment was basically driven underground.

In 1781, William Herschel discovered Uranus. The Vagabond Act of 1824 officially outlawed the practice of astrology in England. Four years later, Raphael (Robert Gross Smith) published his *Manual of Astrology*. Along with the discovery of Uranus, the discovery of Neptune in 1846 enabled astrologers to resolve some of the old ambiguities of their craft.

By the late nineteenth and early twentieth centuries, Rosicrucians, Theosophists, and other occultists in England and the United States were embracing and promoting the craft, and the revival soon spread into Europe, particularly Germany and France. In 1908, Llewellyn George established a school of astrology in Los Angeles, an early forerunner of the American Federation of Astrologers, and in 1920, Evangeline Adams succeeded in getting astrology legalized in New York.

Pluto's discovery in 1930 further helped solve some age-old astrological questions, and astrological interpretation started to become profoundly influenced by depth psychology, the language of which entered the modern astrological lexi-con. Carl Jung, one of the fathers of modern psychology and a proponent of the theory of archetypes, saw in astrology a mar-velous system of symbols representative of the growth of human personality and consciousness in relation to organic, social, and universal principles. By the 1940s, interest in and acceptance of the craft had become widespread. It continues to grow to this day, as does its study, research, and development among modern astrologers, along with a growing interest within the scientific community.

The development of bodies of knowledge from simple observations to complex yet comprehensible definitions is a long evolutionary process. How the system of astrology with its symbols and associated meanings was actually formulated remains one of the great mysteries of humanity. It can be explained by theories of archetypes and synchronicity, the reli-gious urge, and the like, but other than these broad postula-tions there is really no concrete answer other than it simply happened. Certainly, throughout the ages it has influenced the development of much of humanity's knowledge, including religion, mythology, agriculture, philosophy, medicine, naviga-tion, and modern psychology.

One of the earliest symbols of Christianity, found to this day on Catholic altars, is the sign of Pisces—of two fish, one above the other, facing in opposite directions, in direct duality. In astrological terms, Christ is the avatar of the Piscean Age from which we are currently emerging into the Age of Aquarius. Few of the constellations actually bear any definite resemblance to the signs that they represent. Why is the twelfth constellation identified as a pair of fish? Where, fundamentally, do we get this remarkable and strange knowledge, this language from the stars that somehow makes sense to us? How did the *I Ching* in ancient China and its complex binary mathematics that correspond to a written moral and social code of human action and behavior, as well as being a tool for divination, come into being? What is the provenance of the Tarot? How, ultimately, can we explain these things and the fact that they are valid, that they do, indeed, explain both the mysterious and the mundane and provide us with a way of ordering and understanding our experience and coming to terms with ourselves? In Jungian or archetypal terms, the answer is deceptively simple: that they were always there, innate and sublime, simply waiting to be discovered.

THE GREAT ZODIACAL AGES

Beyond the yearly and daily cycles, astrology also accounts for humanity's progression through the aeons, the phases of our evolution, and the development of consciousness. This is seen in the twelve great zodiacal ages, each lasting about 2160 years and forming part of what is known as the "precession of the equinoxes," which is the gradual displacement of the stars in relation to where the Sun crosses the equator at each equinox. The entire cycle lasts 25,920 years and then repeats itself just like the yearly zodiac. The sequence, however, moves in the opposite direction. While the yearly zodiac moves counterclockwise, the ages move clockwise. The age of Aries, the era incorporating the Old Testament, was followed by the age of Pisces, not Taurus, which preceded the Arian Age. At present, we are emerging out of the Piscean Age into the new Age of Aquarius.

The Arian Age was one of iron, conquest, individuality, and city-states. Pisces became a time of great sacrifice, mysticism, and suffering, attributes associated with that sign. The new age that we are entering, that of Aquarius (called by some the age of humanity), implies an age of intellectual growth—of information, science and technology, and global communication—a greatly increased world population, and the solving of complex problems. Aviation and space exploration, computers, and the Internet are obvious heralds of the new age that is dawning.

The age of Aquarius will be followed by the age of Capricorn, in which it is believed things will take on a highly pragmatic orientation, according to Capricorn's earth-sign proclivities. Some astrologers fear it will take on that sign's darker aspects and be an age of impersonal, authoritarian order, and maybe even an age of robots.

THE HOROSCOPE

A horoscope, or natal chart, is, literally, a map of the position of the planets at the exact time and place of a person's birth. It is a circle of 360 degrees, representing the path of the Earth's orbit around the Sun. In the horoscope, this path, or ecliptic, is divided into twelve sections of 30 degrees, each containing one of the Sun signs, the twelve signs of the Zodiac that indicate the Earth's relationship to the Sun's position at the time of your birth. For instance, if you were born in late March or early April, the Sun would have been in the first sign, Aries, making Aries your "Sun sign."

The Zodiac is delineated by the vernal equinox, which is marked by the Sun's position around March 20 of each year,

Table 1: Sun Signs and Corresponding Dates

Glyph	Sign	Dates
♈	Aries	March 21–April 20
♉	Taurus	April 21–May 21
♊	Gemini	May 22–June 21
♋	Cancer	June 22–July 23
♌	Leo	July 24–August 23
♍	Virgo	August 24–September 23
♎	Libra	September 24–October 23
♏	Scorpio	October 24–November 22
♐	Sagittarius	November 23–December 21
♑	Capricorn	December 22–January 20
♒	Aquarius	January 21–February 18
♓	Pisces	February 19–March 20

when the days and nights are equal in length. This occurs when the Sun moves from a position south of the equator to a position north of the equator that is referred to in astrology as 0 degrees Aries. It marks the beginning of the "tropical Zodiac," the Zodiac most commonly used in Western astrology and the only one we shall study here.

The signs of the Zodiac follow an unchanging pattern or progression: Aries, Taurus, Gemini, Cancer, Leo, Virgo, Libra,

Scorpio, Sagittarius, Capricorn, Aquarius, and Pisces. The Zodiac (from the Greek *zoë*, meaning "life," and *diakos*, meaning "wheel") is the Wheel of Life symbolically conceived by the human mind. Table 1 shows the approximate dates of the Sun's annual transit through the signs. You'll find descriptions of the Sun in each of the twelve signs in part 2, beginning on page 91.

Born on the Cusp

The Sun can never be in two signs at once. The "dividing line" between the signs is called the cusp. If you were born at the beginning of a sign and the end of another, you are said to be born on the cusp. The term "cusp" refers both to the boundary line between two signs and the beginning of a horoscopic house. For most astrologers, an individual is considered to be born on the cusp only if the Sun is within three to five degrees, on either side, of a sign. For example, if the Sun was between 25 degrees of Scorpio and 5 degrees of Sagittarius when you were born, it would be considered as being on the Scorpio/Sagittarius cusp. You would be influenced, to some degree, by a blending or overlap of the two signs, like the blending and emergence of colors on the spectrum, with the actual Sun sign in which you are born being the major influence or dominant "color." The Sun sign is apt to find its strongest expression of the sign's characteristics at around 15 degrees of the zodiacal house. For individuals born on or near a cusp, it is necessary to compute the horoscope mathematically to determine the Sun sign. To do so requires not only the month and day but also the year, the time (to the minute, if possible), and place of birth.

OVERVIEW OF THE
HOUSES OF THE HOROSCOPE

We all have the twelve signs of the Zodiac included in our horoscopes. Their influence on the various aspects of our lives is determined by the position of the planets in the signs and the interaction between the signs and the houses of the horoscope.

In addition to containing the twelve signs, the horoscope is divided into twelve houses, with each house related to a sign of the Zodiac, indicated in figure 1 on page 20. While the signs are defined by the Earth's revolution around the Sun, the houses are defined by the Earth's 24-hour rotation on its axis. The houses are also delineated by cusps. The 1st House cusp is found by calculating the point where the eastern horizon is positioned in the horoscope at the time and place of birth and is called the Ascendant, or rising sign. For instance, if you were born on June 7, 1965, at 11:47 AM in Kyoto, Japan, your Sun sign would be Cancer and your Ascendant, the sign rising on your eastern horizon, would be Libra.

Whereas the Sun sign describes your deepest self, your heart or emotional and spiritual essence, the Ascendant describes your early environment and your persona—your personality, appearance (especially the head), and manner of self-expression, your outer mask. Certain astrologers who believe in reincarnation (as did Pythagoras, the father of numerology) see the Ascendant as representative of the individual's efforts and purpose in a past life. The rising sign is the primary manifestation of self-awareness and expression, identity, personality, and self-interest.

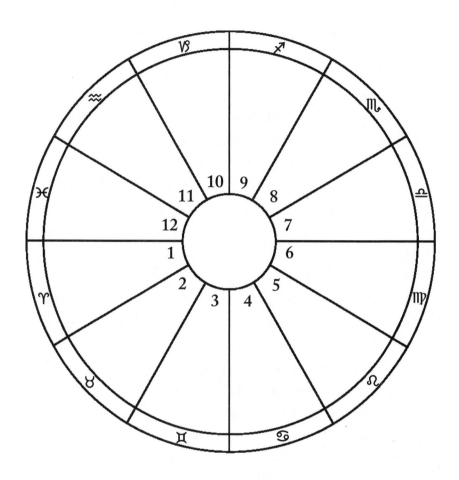

*Fig. 1. The horoscope, showing the "natural" placement
of the Zodiac in the twelve houses.*

The 1st House is naturally followed by the rest of the twelve houses in their fixed order (if Libra is your 1st House, then Scorpio is your 2nd, Sagittarius, your 3rd, and so on). Each of the houses represents various aspects of your life: self, money, communication, home, marriage, work, friendships, obstacles, allies, hopes, desires, and so forth. Each house cusp has a sign of the Zodiac, and these signs describe the influences upon the area of life represented by the particular house. We will go further into the symbolism of the houses in chapter 3.

ZODIACAL QUARTERS

Before we venture into descriptions of the zodiacal signs and their meanings, a brief discussion of the zodiacal quarters and their quadrants in the twelve houses is here appropriate for your overall understanding.

The first quarter, made up of Aries, Taurus, and Gemini (corresponding to spring), represents individuality and personal matters, basic resources, stimulation, and the birth of ideas. These are the 1st, 2nd, and 3rd houses. The second quarter (summer), consisting of Cancer, Leo, and Virgo, consists of the 4th, 5th, and 6th houses and represents that stage in which individual resources are solidified, developed, and refined. In the third, or autumnal, quarter of Libra, Scorpio, and Sagittarius, individuality begins to define itself in areas beyond the strictly personal. In this quadrant, as opposed to the first, the resources and ideas of others play an important role in the definition and function of the self. The last zodiacal quarter, that of winter, consists of Capricorn, Aquarius, and

Pisces. The accumulated knowledge and experience of the three previous quarters find expression in these last three signs. Here is synthesis, fruition, realization, and actualization of all that has come before. In this last quarter, also, are the seeds of the beginning of the new cycle that is about to follow.

THE SIGNS AND THEIR ELEMENTS

According to Empedocles, a Greek philosopher, scientist, and healer who lived in Sicily in the fifth century B.C.E., all matter is comprised of four elements: earth, air, fire, and water. Fire and air are upward and outward reaching elements, whereas earth and water turn inward and downward. In his *Tetrasomia*, or *Doctrine of the Four Elements*, Empedocles described these elements not only as physical manifestations or material substances, but also as spiritual essences. He associated these elements with four gods and goddesses: air with Zeus, earth with Hera, fire with Hades, and water with Nestis (believed to be Persephone, the goddess of the Underworld). His ideas were further developed by Aristotle. As a result, each of the twelve signs of the Zodiac was assigned to one of the four elements.

Carl G. Jung, one of the founders of modern psychology, studied mystical literature, astrology, and alchemy. His theory of intuition, sensation, thinking, and feeling as the four basic components of personality is clearly a derivation of Empedocles' ancient theories about fire, earth, air, and water. Jung focused initially on the polarities of introversion (directing one's attention inward toward thoughts, feelings, and awareness) and extroversion (directing one's energy outward toward people, actions, and external objects).

In astrology, each of the four elements governs three signs, which form a triad. The three signs belonging to the same element are basically harmonious with each other and share similar characteristics in terms of personality, intellect, and innate sensibility. The categories are:

Fire: Aries, Leo, and Sagittarius
Earth: Taurus, Virgo, and Capricorn
Air: Gemini, Libra, and Aquarius
Water: Cancer, Scorpio, and Pisces

Fire and air signs are said to be masculine, or *yang*. Water and earth signs are feminine, or *yin*, although it may be more accurate to classify air signs as yang-yin and earth signs as yin-yang, as these two elements tend to share more androgynous qualities.

In general terms, the elements represent basic functions or processes that characterize the signs that belong to them: fire corresponds to intuition; earth, to sensation, reason, and empirical observation; air, to thinking; and water, to feeling.

The Fire Signs: Aries, Leo, and Sagittarius

Each of the fire signs represents aspects of the self or ego in relation to self-expression and creativity that are intuitive in nature and based on internal impulses, the drive to define and manifest the individual self. Aries seeks to impress others and to be admired for its willful tenacity and resolve. Leo seeks and needs an audience for its dramatic self-expression, one in which the various qualities of its character will find an effective response. Sagittarius is driven to expand its horizons, to seek self-realization through active participation with others.

When negative, fire signs can be egotistical, stubborn, aggressive, and prone to fits of temper.

The Earth Signs: Taurus, Virgo, and Capricorn

The earth signs are the most practical of the four types and are associated with the senses and the empirical gathering of data. Their view of the world tends to be pragmatic, with a concern for what is tangible and concrete. Defining, placing, and working within practical limits is one of their primary tasks, and as a result they are devoted to their work and imbued with a strong sense of duty and responsibility. When negative, they can show a tendency to be overly materialistic, neurotic about trivial details and order, and unable to comprehend and embrace new ideas.

In terms of the ideal, Taurus works for itself and personal gain, relying on its own resources and talents. Virgo works for others, utilizing their skills to augment its own. And Capricorn works for society or mankind as a whole.

The Air Signs: Gemini, Libra, and Aquarius

The air signs represent various phases and forms of personal and social interrelationships. They are associated with communication, intellectual activity, and social agreements, customs, and manners. The air signs are primarily concerned with mental abilities and intellectual attributes in one form or another.

In Gemini, this intellectualism shows itself as an ability to obtain, utilize, and communicate factual information. In Libra, these qualities are used to weigh, balance, and make comparisons, while in Aquarius we see an intuitive grasp of principles and ideas and how they apply to the general welfare of humanity. When negative, air signs can be mercurial, indecisive, and mentally fragmented.

The Water Signs: Cancer, Scorpio, and Pisces

The water signs are associated with the subconscious, with feelings and psychic forces. They are receptive and able to penetrate the hidden meanings of life's mysteries. Protective by nature, they are able to shelter others, relieve suffering, and provide the necessities of life.

Cancer is the mother and the home. Scorpio is the mutual exchange and support that occurs in close relationships, with strong feelings about joint resources, death, and the occult mysteries of life. Pisces represents the altruistic care of others, nourishment on the broadest possible scale, strong mystical feelings about the Infinite, and the unconscious ability to communicate telepathically with others.

When negative, the water signs can be excessively emotional, insular, secretive, possessive, and capable of using their considerable powers of empathy and psychic receptivity to beguile and manipulate others.

THE SIGNS AND THEIR QUALITIES

In addition to the four elements that form three triads, the signs are further classified into three qualities of four signs each: *cardinal*, or initiating; *fixed*, or synthesizing; and *mutable*, or modifying. These are:

Cardinal: Aries, Cancer, Libra, and Capricorn
Fixed: Taurus, Leo, Scorpio, and Aquarius
Mutable: Gemini, Virgo, Sagittarius, and Pisces

The four signs of each quality are of different elements (we could say psychology), but they share in a complementary purpose, distinct from one another yet part of the same process, like the four seasons. The four signs of each quality form a mandala, or cosmic cross. These crosses represent three basic areas of experience, learning, and growth, the crosses that we all must bear in what is known as the "process of individuation," of becoming and being.

Corresponding to the solstices and the equinoxes is the cardinal cross of Aries, Cancer, Libra, and Capricorn. It begins with fire and ends with earth. The second, the fixed cross of Taurus, Leo, Scorpio, and Aquarius, begins with earth and ends with air. The third, the mutable cross of Gemini, Virgo, Sagittarius, and Pisces, begins with air and concludes in water. The deep waters of Pisces, the last sign of the Zodiac, contain the basic elements of life that spring forth in the sign immediately following it, Aries, the sign of the fire of individuality (and of spring), of the *I am what am*, the beginning of the new cycle, the start of a new turn of the Great Wheel. In this sense, Pisces is not only the end, but also the beginning.

The Cardinal Signs:
Aries, Cancer, Libra, and Capricorn

The cardinal signs are associated with creation, initiation, action, challenge, trial, burdens, support, influence, and strength. Aries is selfhood and the desire for its immediate expression and expansion. Cancer is security, foundation, and depth. Libra is concerned with relationships and breadth, while Capricorn is the attainment of goals and height. These signs represent the role of the individual in public affairs and social conflicts. Their power is apparent, overt, and exoteric rather than covert and esoteric. Their primary impulses are directed toward individual security and freedom.

Aries and Libra have to do with individuality and its striving to broaden its horizons and find a complementary partner, of the self coming to meet the other, of individual expansion, projection, exploration, and discovery. Cancer and Capricorn are the maternal and paternal, respectively. Cancer is the home and the mother—insular, nurturing, and protective. Capricorn is the father, his means of provision, and the rules of society that ensure his position in it and its order and success.

The Fixed Signs:
Taurus, Leo, Scorpio, and Aquarius

Keywords associated with the fixed signs are empowerment, execution, order, direction, experience, accumulation, insemination, evaluation, and endurance. Taurus acquires and utilizes the energies and materials at its direct disposal. Leo expresses itself intuitively and dramatically in the name of some cause or enterprise. Scorpio is adept at using the resources of others, particularly those of a mate or partner for their mutual benefit. Aquarius provides the form and currency of communication and ideas that benefit friends and associations bound by common interests. These signs are concerned with shared resources, experiences, and rewards, as well as losses. They signify the ideas, values, people, and things that are of fundamental importance in the individual quest for affirmation and self-actualization in society as a whole.

Taurus and Scorpio, complementary signs, deal with the accumulation and disposal of resources. Each reminds the other of their mutual but opposite purpose. Leo and Aquarius face the problems of self-expression, as a singular individual as Leo and in relationships and partnerships as Aquarius.

The Mutable Signs:
Gemini, Virgo, Sagittarius, and Pisces

The mutable signs, according to some astrologers, are the product of a later development in the original Zodiac from eight to twelve signs. They represent concepts of no interest to the so-called "common man." Mutability has become associated with a certain flexible high-mindedness and transcendence beyond the concerns of self-actualization, attainment, and power. Among the keywords for the mutable signs are refinement, adjustment, dissemination, assistance, rescue, repair, review, application, compassion, understanding, suffering, self-sacrifice, and utilization. The mutable mindset is interested in pursuing and refining the ideas set in motion by the cardinal and fixed signs. It develops rather than creates and in so doing plants the seed from which the cardinal and fixed signs can begin once again to create anew. The power of the mutable signs is based on the accumulated achievements and knowledge of the cardinal and fixed signs. It is covert and esoteric, based on reason and judgment of all that has come before it. Its discoveries, revelations, and innovations find their expression in the cardinal sign that follow it, referring us back to the Pisces-Aries relationship I mentioned earlier. The mutable signs represent the final stage in the development of our basic drives and values toward a higher ideal on the physical, mental, emotional, and spiritual planes. The mutable signs take the inspiration of the cardinal signs and the concrete boundaries of the fixed signs and refine and expand them with a view to the future.

Gemini and Sagittarius are concerned with the intellect, the accumulation and relationship of ideas, and journeying into new and foreign realms, both physically and mentally. They are the travelers, concerned with mobility and learning. Gemini acquires information, and Sagittarius takes it and expands upon it, infusing it with new ideas and insights gleaned along the way. Gemini is the wandering minstrel, the vagabond poet collecting stories to tell, while Sagittarius is the serious explorer, traveling with a lot more luggage and equipment and sedulously making notes. Virgo is the traveling merchant, filled with practical and commercial goals, the Marco Polo of the Zodiac, and Pisces is the pilgrim on the solitary, holy journey. Each has a remarkable story to tell. The role of the mutable signs is to serve, aid, heal, and support, to give rather than take. The mandala or cross formed by these four signs is that of self-understanding and self-sacrifice, of Buddha's suffering and enlightenment, and Christ's crucifixion for his ideals—based on the fixed signs' principles of love, spiritual freedom, and sharing—upon the cardinal cross of established authority.

CHAPTER 2

THE PLANETS

The planets can be viewed as core components of the personality that is expressed by the signs in which they are found. An understanding of the personality traits that each planet represents, coupled with what you have learned about the signs, will help you build a basic picture of the personality represented by the horoscope. In this chapter, we will explore the qualities of each planet including its "dignities," which help you determine the strength of the planet's influence in the horoscope, and its mythology. We will also learn what it means when a planet is "afflicted."

THE SUN AND THE MOON
☉ ☽

Both the Sun and the Moon are of primary importance in astrological analysis. The Sun represents our vital force, conscious purpose, and self-expression. It denotes our essential character and convictions. It is associated with the masculine, the active or yang principle—the father, consciousness, and solar light or radiance.

The Moon indicates our emotional responses to life's situations, the attitudes instilled by family and early childhood, and how those formative experiences color our emotional outlook. It represents attitudes toward women in general, domestic and daily life, and eating habits and preferences. It represents the threshold of the unconscious, inherited traits, survival instincts, sentiments, emotional attachments, and empathy with one's environment. It reflects the rapidly changing or fluctuating moods we are subject to, the daily ebb and flow of the tides. It is the feminine, receptive, or yin principle—mother, nourishment, shelter, security, fecundity, and family tradition. The Moon passes through a sign approximately every two days.

MERCURY
☿

Mercury in a sign describes the means by which we communicate and adapt to daily life. Mercury shows how the characteristics of the sign it's located in influence thinking and communication, the way all creative powers of the individual are manifested and directed. Mercury is the ruler of the thinking process, and its sign position reveals the psychological patterns and perceptions that determine the ability to make judgments and decisions and convey ideas to others, as well as the areas of concern that are of primary importance to the particular individual. Mercury takes roughly 365 days to move through the Zodiac and is rarely far from the sign in which the Sun is located. If it's not in the same sign as the Sun, it's usually in either the sign preceding or following the Sun.

VENUS
♀

Venus is more or less an indicator of the type of ideal mate or partner to whom we are likely to be attracted. Venus in the signs shows how we express our emotions in love and marriage. It can also provide insight into attitudes about money, personal possessions, creature comforts, and aesthetic and social values. Like Mercury, Venus also travels along with the Sun, making its transit through the Zodiac in about 225 days. Venus can be as far as two signs away from the Sun sign.

MARS
♂

Mars is an indicator of the nature of our personal drives and energies. The position of Mars reveals far more about our actual sex drive or libido than does Venus. The sign in which it's found describes the way we act when motivated by our desire. It also describes the nature of our ambition and the type of work we are inclined to do. Desire, impulsive action, and assertive energy can lead into danger, and the position of Mars can also imply the type of danger and violence we may encounter or generate. Mars takes roughly two to two and a half years to move through all the signs of the Zodiac.

JUPITER
♃

Jupiter embodies our ideals. Jupiter's position shows the nature of our moral, religious, and philosophical beliefs. It shows how we express generosity and sharing and what benefits we receive in return. It indicates not only where we are likely to receive financial and material benefits, but also how we have earned the goodwill of others. Jupiter, as coruler of Pisces (see page 37 for a discussion on planetary rulerships), shows the means by which we receive the karmic rewards for past good deeds, as well how we manifest our compassion and generosity toward those less fortunate. Jupiter takes about twelve years to make a complete cycle through the Zodiac.

SATURN

♄

Saturn indicates the areas of strong personal responsibilities. Saturn is actually referred to by some astrologers as "the grim reaper," but it's probably more helpful to look at Saturn as the cosmic teacher. It takes twenty-nine years to complete its cycle through the Zodiac. Saturn shows the ways in which we must take responsibility and learn the importance of discipline and working positively within life's limitations, which give concrete shape to being and things on the earthly plane. It shows the burdens that we must carry and the lessons we must learn. It also indicates the kind of work to which we are suited. Saturn's position shows where we are most likely to experience difficulties and limitations and how an idea is physically actualized through willpower, patience, and hard work. The affairs ruled by the sign in which Saturn is placed will tend to take on a particularly serious nature. These are those areas and aspects of life in which we learn to cope with life's travails in order to make a successful living. Here, obstacles are overcome on the path of becoming, and we come into our own. Saturn's placement in the horoscope is a strong indicator of the nature of our career path, the kind of work we will do, and the hardships and tests we will go through in order to climb the mountain to recognition and status.

URANUS
♅

Uranus in the horoscope shows the ways in which our urge for individuality and freedom are manifested. It indicates the motivations behind our hopes, desires, and goals, especially those envisioned by the mind. The sign occupied by Uranus describes not only our friends but also those social areas of life where we take dynamic action and instigate change. Uranus in the signs shows how we receive and interpret inspiration and original ideas from the collective and universal consciousness and set upon solving life's puzzles and problems. Uranus takes seven years to pass through one sign of the Zodiac, so that everyone born within the same seven-year period has Uranus in the same sign, although the individual house position will vary. The sign position of Uranus (and even more so Neptune and Pluto) is an important indicator of generational differences and the shared destiny, concerns, and mores of a large group of people, of the *zeitgeist* of the times in which they are born and what they will collectively set in motion. The sign position has more historical than personal significance. As with the other "outer planets"—Neptune and Pluto—Uranus's sign position is less important than its house position in denoting our personality and proclivities in regard to the affairs, attitudes, and actions ruled by the planet.

NEPTUNE
♆

Neptune takes approximately 164 years to pass through a complete cycle of the Zodiac. It spends about thirteen years in each sign. Thus, the sign in which Neptune is located has more of a generational significance than it does personal. Neptune in the signs shows the kind of shared cultural expression that will be indicative of those born within the same thirteen-year period.

The sign Neptune is in tells us something about where seclusion and solitude will be sought as well as the cultural and creative expression of a particular generation.

PLUTO
♇

Pluto is the slowest moving of the planets, taking approximately 248 years to make a complete transit through the Zodiac. It has an eccentric orbit, which means that the number of years it spends in each sign varies from twelve to thirty-two. Along with Uranus and Neptune, its sign position is more of a historical and generational indicator than a personal one. The sign positions of Pluto are of great historical significance, as it is the planet of drastic and fundamental movements and upheavals that bring about great historical and cultural change.

These changes can be positive or negative, regenerative or degenerative, representative either of the principle of Eros (life-affirming relating) or the principle of Thanatos (death). Often, both effects are felt at the same time, producing extremes of good and evil, life and death, in the arena ruled by the particular sign. For example, the atomic bomb ended the Second World War while Pluto was in Leo. Pluto in the signs always brings about a radical and permanent transformation that effects the whole of civilization. On the personal level, Pluto shows us how we are connected to our generation through the values, mores, and social attitudes it adheres to.

PLANETARY RULERSHIP

The planet whose characteristics have the strongest affinity with the attributes of a particular sign is said to be that sign's ruler. The ruler of a horoscopic house is the planet that rules the sign appearing on the beginning, or cusp, of the house (see chapter 3 for a complete discussion of the houses). *Sun sign ruler* refers to the planet that rules your birth sign. The ruler of the horoscope as a whole is considered by most astrologers to be the planet ruling the sign appearing at the beginning of the 1st House—the Ascendant, or rising sign. With the discovery of the outer planets Uranus, Neptune, and Pluto, several signs were assigned new rulers. Table 2 on page 38 lists the signs and their modern and traditional ruling planets.

There is still some disagreement about the rulers of certain signs, and some astrologers continue to adhere to the traditional rulerships.

Table 2. Planetary Rulerships.

Sign	Modern Ruler	Traditional Ruler
Aries	Mars	Mars
Taurus	Venus	Venus
Gemini	Mercury	Mercury
Cancer	Moon	Moon
Leo	Sun	Sun
Virgo	Mercury	Mercury
Libra	Venus	Venus
Scorpio	Pluto	Mars
Sagittarius	Jupiter	Jupiter
Capricorn	Saturn	Saturn
Aquarius	Uranus	Saturn
Pisces	Neptune	Jupiter

PLANETARY DIGNITIES

Each planet has two signs (or four, in the case of planets with dual rulership) in which it is "comfortable" and two in which it is not. In the horoscope, when a planet is found in the sign that it rules, it is said to be in *dignity*, and it is at its most potent expression.

When a planet appears in the second sign in which it expresses itself harmoniously, it is said to be in *exaltation.*

If a planet is found in the sign opposite of the one that it rules, or in which it is dignified, it is said to be in *detriment.* The planet is not able to work at its full potential and takes on more of the sign's attributes than its own. A person with a planet in detriment may feel that energy as being in a place where he or she has to follow someone else's game plan.

When a planet is found in the sign opposite the sign of its exaltation, the planet is said to be in *fall.* Here, the native will have difficulty expressing the planet's essential attributes.

When a planet is in a house of which it is the natural ruler—for example, Venus in the 7th House, or the Sun in the 5th—it is said to be in *accidental dignity*, or dignity by house. This is the house in which it is most comfortable and therefore is more visible as an active part of the native's life path. Table 3 on pages 40–41 shows the signs of the dignities for each planet. The signs appearing in parentheses are in those dignities according to the traditional rulerships (see table 2).

Table 3. Planetary Dignities.

Planet	Dignity	Detriment
☉ Sun	♌ Leo	♒ Aquarius
☽ Moon	♋ Cancer	♑ Capricorn
☿ Mercury	♊ (♍) Gemini (Virgo)	♐ (♓) Sagittarius (Pisces)
♀ Venus	♉ (♎) Taurus (Libra)	♏ (♈) Scorpio (Aries)
♂ Mars	♈ (♏) Aries (Scorpio)	♎ (♉) Libra (Taurus)
♃ Jupiter	♐ (♓) Sagittarius (Pisces)	♓ (♍) Gemini (Virgo)
♄ Saturn	♑ (♒) Capricorn (Aquarius)	♋ (♌) Cancer (Leo)
♅ Uranus	♒ Aquarius	♌ Leo
♆ Neptune	♓ Pisces	♍ Virgo
♇ Pluto	♏ Scorpio	♉ Taurus

Table 3. Planetary Dignities, cont.

Exaltation	Fall	By House
♈ Aries	♎ Libra	5th
♉ Taurus	♏ Scorpio	4th
♒ Aquarius	♌ Leo	3rd & 6th
♓ Pisces	♍ Virgo	2nd & 7th
♑ Capricorn	♋ Cancer	1st
♋ Cancer	♑ Capricorn	9th
♎ Libra	♈ Aries	10th
♏ Scorpio	♉ Taurus	11th
Not yet known.	Not yet known.	12th
Not yet known.	Not yet known.	8th

When you study the planetary dignities along with the qualities of the signs, you can see how the nature of a planet is either dampened or invigorated by the sign it's in. For example, Saturn, the planet of limitation, clashes with the impulsive, devil-may-care Aries energy. Jupiter, the planet of expansion, is constricted in Capricorn, the sign of measured progress. Uranus, the planet of freedom and innovation, finds full expression in the penetrating and uncompromising insight of Scorpio.

Looking at Marlon Brando's chart as an example (see figure 6, page 57), his natal Sun, Venus, and Mars are exalted in Aries, Taurus, and Capricorn, respectively. These three planetary positions are powerful in his chart, indicating a highly creative person who is able to easily express his essence (Sun) and channel it through his considerable drive (Mars) to support his values, relationships, and what pleases him (Venus). His Ascendant is in Sagittarius; therefore, the ruler of his chart is Sagittarius's ruling planet, Jupiter, which is also in dignity in Sagittarius. So, in addition to clearly exhibiting the qualities of his Sun, Moon, and Mars, Brando's personality has a marked Jupiterian nature—highly philosophical, generous, and expansive. With Jupiter in the 1st House, which indicates one's physical presence (see chapter 3), we can see how Brando, in addition to being a larger-than-life person, also had a propensity toward weight gain.

WHEN A PLANET IS "AFFLICTED"

A planet is considered to be afflicted when it is placed in a sign of its detriment or fall, in a house in which it finds difficulty expressing itself, or when it forms a challenging aspect, such as the square or opposition (see chapter 4 on aspects), with Mars, Saturn, Uranus, Neptune, or Pluto. Weak house placements for the Sun, for example, would be in the houses ruled by the signs of its detriment (Aquarius) or fall (Libra), the 11th and 7th Houses, respectively. In Marlon Brando's chart, his Aries Moon could be considered afflicted by the squares it forms to Mars in Capricorn and Pluto in Cancer. On the other hand, the influences of the carefully enduring Capricorn Mars and deeply nurturing Cancerian Pluto in his chart may have had a tempering effect on the impulsive, emotionally self-involved, and demanding nature of his Aries Moon. Furthermore, Brando's Moon is in accidental dignity in the 4th House, where its expression finds support.

CHAPTER 3

THE TWELVE
HOROSCOPIC HOUSES

A s was stated in the first chapter, a horoscope is a diagram of the solar system in relation to a specific time and place of birth and is made up of twelve sections called the houses. The signs are reckoned by the Sun's annual transit through the four seasons, while the houses are figured by the daily rotation of the Earth on its axis. The planets "transit," or pass through the signs, and the signs and the planets are located within the houses. There is a correspondence between the twelve signs and the twelve houses, due to the elements and qualities they have in common (refer to figure 1 on page 20, which shows the "natural chart," with the corresponding signs placed on each house cusp). Aries, the first sign, corresponds to the 1st House, but owing to the daily rotation of the Earth, Aries corresponds to approximately two hours of the 1st-House influence. A new sign, that of Taurus, will rise on the cusp of the 1st House within two hours. Within twenty-four hours, each sign will have passed through all of the twelve houses.

The wheel of the houses is divided into four hemispheres: eastern, western, southern, and northern, each made up of six houses. These are seen as four quarters, or quadrants. The most important houses are known as the *angular* houses; they correspond to the cardinal signs and are therefore sometimes referred to as *cardinal*. The cardinal houses are the 1st House (the Ascendant or Rising Sign), the 4th House cusp (also known as the Nadir, or the IC—*Imum Coeli*—the "lowest heavens," where the plane of the meridian passes underneath the Earth and intersects the ecliptic), the 7th House cusp (or Descendent, the point where the meridian passes beneath the Earth and intersects the western horizon ecliptic), and the 10th House or Midheaven (often indicated as the MC, *Medium Colei*, or "highest heavens"). The Midheaven is the point where the meridian, passing from north to south through a point directly overhead (the zenith), intersects the plane of the ecliptic. The other eight houses are spaced between these four angular house cusps.

The 1st House is significant in that it refers to our core being more than the other houses. The houses become increasingly impersonal as they proceed from the 1st to the 12th. The nature of the Rising Sign is modified by the horoscope as a whole, especially by the positions and aspects affecting the planet ruling the Ascendant, the Sun, the Moon, and any other planets located within the 1st House close to the Ascendant. Quite often Mars, more than any other planet, has an important bearing upon the Ascendant, for it has a natural affinity with the 1st House because of its rulership over Aries, the first sign of the Zodiac and the correspondence of that sign with the 1st House.

The cusps of the four angular houses—the 1st, 4th, 7th, and 10th—correspond to 6:00 AM, midnight, 6:00 PM, and noon, respectively (see figure 2, below). Every four minutes mark a new degree of the Zodiac to the cusp of the 1st House, the Ascendant. Looking at the horoscopic wheel, the four directions are the reverse of the clock. The 1st House is the eastern horizon; the 4th is the northern sector; the 7th, the western horizon; the 10th, the southern sector.

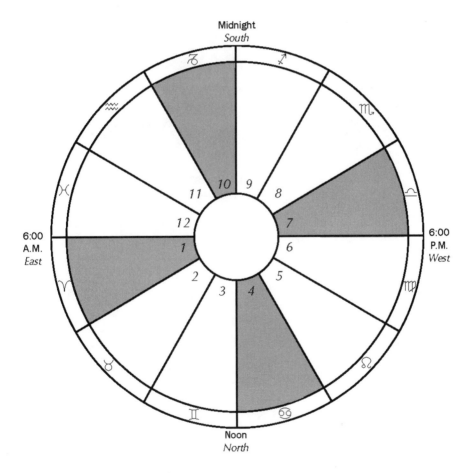

Fig. 2. The angular, or cardinal houses.

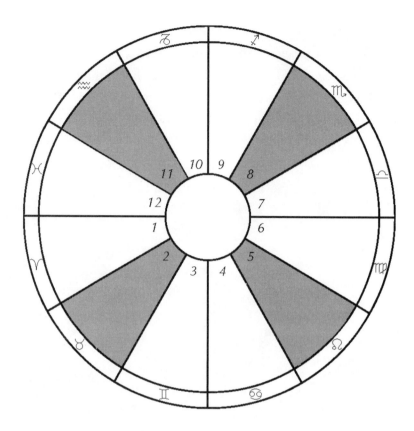

Fig. 3. The succedent houses.

The 2nd, 5th, 8th, and 11th Houses, which follow the car-
dinals, are called the *succedent* houses and have a strong affinity with the fixed signs (see figure 3, above).

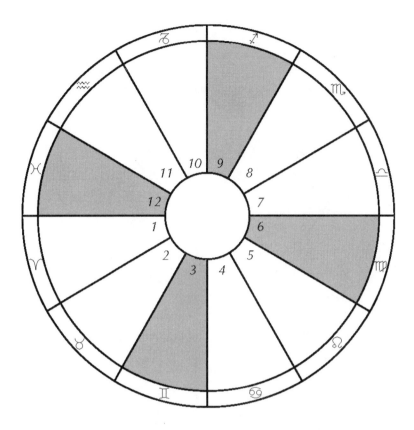

Fig. 4. The cadent houses.

The third group of houses, known as the *cadent* houses—the 3rd, 6th, 9th, and 12th—correspond to the mutable signs (see figure 4, above).

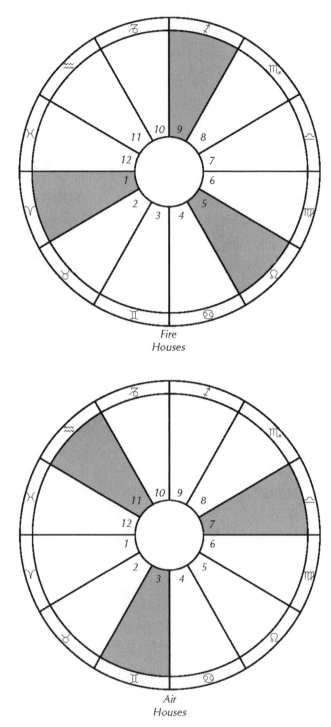

Fire
Houses

Air
Houses

Fig. 5. The houses and their elements.

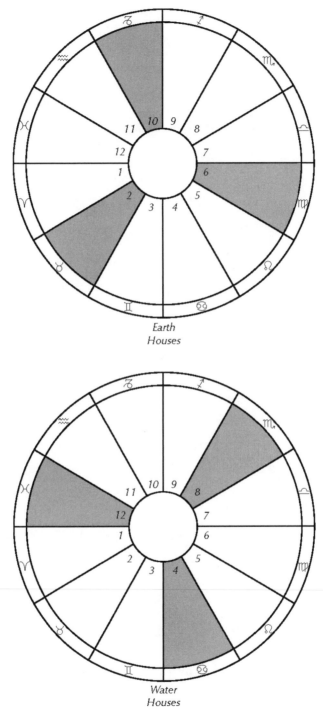

Fig. 5. *The houses and their elements, cont.*

In terms of the elements, the 1st, 5th, and 9th Houses are related to the fire signs. The 2nd, 6th, and 10th are associated with the earth signs; the 3rd, 7th, and 11th, with the air signs; the 4th, 8th, and 12th with the water signs (see figure 5, pages 50–51).

THE FOUR HEMISPHERES

The eastern hemisphere of the Zodiac, which includes the 10th, 11th, 12th, 1st, 2nd, and 3rd Houses, represents our projection of the self into the public sphere where there is effective exchange and communication with others and we glean personal rewards.

The opposite side of the wheel, the western hemisphere, which includes the 4th, 5th, 6th, 7th, 8th, and 9th Houses, relates to familial and social relationships, marriage, partnerships, and formal social ties. Here, the need for cooperation and tact in achieving our aims, working with others, and the need for balance between personal feelings and attachments and the social requirements of adapting to others are emphasized.

Below the horizon of the wheel, the 1st through 6th Houses make up the northern hemisphere, representing personal issues related to childhood, the family, and the clan. These are the values and skills we learned at an early age from our family, friends, and society, and their influence on our abilities for creative self-expression. The role of the mother and early family life and environment are emphasized here. In the eastern hemisphere, the emphasis is on the expression of individual will; in the western half, cooperation and formal or objective relationships with others are represented. In the northern hemisphere, we see the emotional foundations for survival.

The last hemisphere, the southern, is concerned with less subjective aspects than the northern. It is social and public rather than personal and familial. When we have a majority of planets in the 7th, 8th, 9th, 10th, 11th, and 12th Houses, the indication is that we may well reach public prominence or celebrity in some way. Here, we see the personal drive for power, recognition, honor, and influence, whether for good or bad. This is the hemisphere where we are most visible—and vulnerable—to the public eye. Those aspects associated with the father (career, ambition, authority, law, and honor) are determining factors, in contrast to the insular and matriarchal concerns of the opposite hemisphere, where the emphasis is on nourishment.

The planet that most accurately represents the southern hemisphere is Saturn; Mars the eastern hemisphere; the Moon the northern hemisphere; and Venus the western. This is due to the fact that these are also the natural rulers of the four angular, or cardinal, houses (the 10th, 1st, 4th, and 7th, respectively), which form the basic framework for the other houses of the horoscope. This quaternary principle is the archetype by which we give order to reality. There are four seasons, four cardinal directions, four elements, four sides to a pyramid, and four psychological types.

The planets and the signs they occupy in a hemisphere show what struggles an individual must go through in order to realize his or her full potential. The signs in the hemispheres change by six houses each day. A new sign appears on the eastern horizon approximately every two hours, altering the overall picture. Therefore, two people born twelve hours apart on the same day and in the same place will have planets in opposite hemispheres. Although their lives will be similar in many ways, one will be more objectively oriented and the other more subjectively inclined.

THE QUADRANTS

The horoscopic wheel is also divided into four quadrants. The first quadrant, consisting of the 1st, 2nd, and 3rd Houses, corresponds to spring and the emergence of individuality. It is here that basic values and ideas are formed. This is the quadrant of greatest spontaneity and individuality, where native intelligence, adaptability, and communication all work for our best interests. It is the quadrant in which we determine what we wish to be in life. Here, also, the mother and early childhood are important formative factors.

The second quadrant, made up of the 4th, 5th, and 6th Houses, shows how we go about producing that which will bring security both to ourselves and our family. It describes the means by which we secure more permanent foundations and establish connections with the family and society. This quadrant is the home and the workplace, those places that are the basis of our security.

In the third quadrant, the 7th, 8th, and 9th Houses, the security sought and established in the second quadrant is extended to include our mate or partner and those with whom we form partnerships. Within this autumnal quadrant are the seeds of fulfillment through finding a suitable complement to our own talents, resources, and desires, both physically and mentally. This is the quadrant of relationships, alliances, and individual expansion into new experiences, where personal horizons are broadened and new challenges are met.

The cusp of the 10th House, the Midheaven, begins the last quadrant. This marks the highest individual achievement we can attain. This is where the Sun would be at noon, at its zenith. In this quadrant, relationships are formed that will further our standing and extend our success as widely as possible. Here is the hope of realizing our aspirations and where objective relationships are more important than personal or subjective ones.

Mars is most like the first quadrant, the Moon like the second, Venus like the third, and Saturn like the fourth. Here are the four seasons of life in which crops are planted, cultivated, harvested, and utilized.

ANGULAR, SUCCEDENT, AND CADENT HOUSES AND LIFE PASSAGES

The angular houses represent the beginning of the four phases of human experience: the individual or personal, the familial or tribal, the social or public, and the universal or cosmopolitan.

In the succedent houses following the angular houses, values are defined, realized, transformed, or adapted to the resources necessary for our growth in each particular quadrant.

The final stage in each quadrant is described by the cadent houses. Here, the impulses described in the angular houses are organized and adapted to satisfy immediate needs, whether they are material gain, friendship, or sexual release. The cadent houses also relate to such matters as communication of values and ideas, the acquisition of practical skills, travel to foreign lands, and compassionate acts for others.

GETTING TO KNOW THE HOUSES

The houses represent the various departments of life. Each house is its own particular arena, and each planet within the house represents an opportunity or a challenge according to the meaning of the house, the planet, and the sign occupying the house. Several planets in a house indicate different levels, phases, or experiences related to the area of life represented by the house.

When there are no planets in a house, you look at the sign appearing on the house cusp and then to the position of the planet ruling the sign; you would also look at where the ruler of the house in the "natural" horoscope is located in the chart and meld all of these symbols into a story. Marlon Brando's chart (figure 6, on page 57) is a great example, because his 7th House, relating to partnerships— which most people want to know about in any astrological consultation—is "empty," and we all know that Brando's love life was certainly not! Gemini is on the cusp of Brando's 7th House, however, and Gemini's ruler, Mercury, is located in the 5th House. The ruler of the "natural" 7th House (the house of Libra) is Venus—in dignity in Taurus—in Brando's 6th house, accounting for his highly

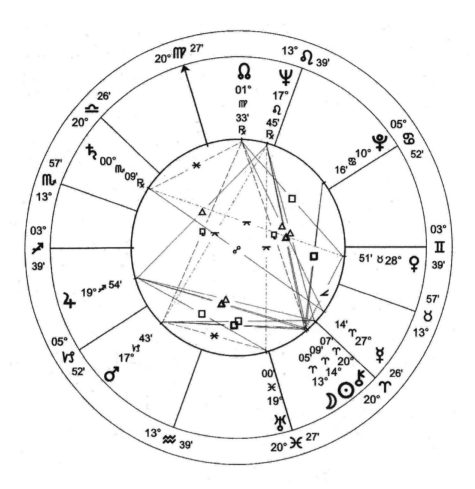

*Fig. 6. Marlon Brando, born April 3, 1924, 11:00 PM CST
Omaha, Nebraska. (Chart provided courtesy of Seven Stars
bookstore using Solar Fire software.)*

sensual appeal in his work. Working with the symbolism of all these elements, you could venture that here was a person inclined to have diverse partnerships (Gemini, 7th House) that would spring from romantic affairs (5th House) in his work (6th House) involving creative self-expression (5th House). Coupled with his Sagittarius (foreign lands, travel) Ascendant (also important regarding marriages, as it opposes the 7th House), you could also venture to guess that his partners would tend to be from a different land. Indeed, none of Brando's three wives were American, each was an actress, and each was pregnant at the time of marriage. How Brando tended to handle these relationships is revealed in the aspects (see chapter 4) formed between the planets. Once you get acquainted with the meaning of the individual houses, you, too, will be able to glimpse the image-story in the astrological symbolism.

The 1st House

 Sign: Aries
Co-Rulers: Mars and Pluto

The 1st House is also the Ascendant. The sign on the cusp of the 1st House is the Rising Sign. It is the most important house cusp and the most sensitive in the horoscope. It is related to Aries and describes the persona, the "I am" of the individual. Thus, the sign rising on the 1st House cusp describes self-awareness, the means and form of self-expression, temperament, and how experiences and stimuli are assimilated, interpreted, and responded to. Self-interest is most readily identified by the sign that is ascending. The 1st House also represents our physical appearance, especially the head and upper part of the face. In the 1st House, instincts and intuition are more important than feelings of empathy (the 4th House) and reason (the 7th House). The 1st House represents the beginning, the formative experiences of early childhood (both good and bad) that help define the personality.

When you're tackling a horoscope interpretation, try to encompass the meanings of the most important indicators of the individual's self—the 1st House and Rising Sign, Mars, Sun, and Moon. While the 1st House, Mars, and the Rising Sign denote the outward persona, the Sun's position indicates the deeper will and sense of purpose. The Moon's position serves to further modify the self as defined by the Sun's position (inner self) and the Rising Sign (outer self).

EXAMPLE

Marlon Brando's chart shows the Sun and Moon in Aries at the time of his birth. Here is the potential to be a natural leader, with thoughts (Sun, consciousness) and feelings (Moon) harmonious with the actions taken. This is a dynamic individual who loves action and is ardent, aggressive, and commanding, and makes others aware of these qualities in himself. These qualities of character are generally beneficial, but at times can cause trouble as a result of impulsiveness, impatience, and the need to prove himself by rushing headlong toward danger.

Furthermore, at the time of Brando's birth, Sagittarius was on the horizon. Sagittarius's ruler, Jupiter, is located in the 1st House, further emphasizing Brando's Sagittarian qualities. Sagittarians project optimism, joviality, friendliness, and a keen interest in the world around them, although they have a tendency to think solely in terms of their own affairs and concerns. They are ambitious on a grand scale, and their power lies in their ability to influence people to think and act in a way that is to their own personal advantage. Although they often take things for granted, their energetic optimism is often a source of inspiration to those around them. Sagittarius rising indicates a life that is very dualistic, divided dramatically into fluctuating situations of success and failure. If his mind can be raised above the common and trivial to more profound subjects and concerns, his intellect will become very philosophical and attracted to law and peace, with an intuitive human understanding that is able to advise and assist others. Here is a life that will be colored by impulsive and stubborn personal tendencies, with an inclination to go to extremes. Brando's involvement with the rights of Native Americans and his refusal to accept an Oscar for his role in *The Godfather* is a manifestation of this energy.

Sagittarius gives a strong love of nature and makes the individual somewhat extroverted, demonstrative, and passionate, falling in love frequently and without reservations. The Sagittarian Ascendant's romantic life is intense and varied, and his lovers may find him difficult to understand. He will appear as passionate and energetic, but as a result of the mutability of the sign, there is also an opposite tendency that leads away from involvement in the love affair due to an inner concern with personal freedom.

The sign of Sagittarius inclines people to exist in environments in which the physical body, emotions, and thoughts are allowed total freedom for development. On a higher, intellectual level there is an inclination to be preoccupied with the deep complexities of philosophy, metaphysics, religion, and law. Versatile and intellectual, this is an individual who requires both intellectual and physical exercise. Brando's total involvement in Method acting was an especially adept use of this Ascendant.

Jupiter in the 1st House indicates that success in life is achieved through personal effort and merit, that dignity and respectability are attained by strength of personality. This individual's temperament is innately honest, truthful, kind, and courageous, projecting spontaneity, frankness, and a benign good humor. The downside of the 1st-House Jupiter is the tendency toward weight gain, as Jupiter is the planet of expansion and the 1st House is related to appearance. Additionally, there is an easy connection (trine, see chapter 4) to his Moon (nurturing) in Aries (impulsiveness), furthering his chances for weight gain. Yet, it is a testament to Jupiter's benevolence that he was able to turn even this seeming "liability" into an asset. Tempering Brando's impulsive, fiery nature is his Mars in Capricorn in the 2nd House, as Capricorn's natural reserve has a restrictive effect on Mars. However, the earthy, enduring nature of Capricorn gives him the steady energy to carry his fire.

The 2nd House

Sign: Taurus
Ruler: Venus

The 2nd House deals with the material resources required to sustain the self as defined in the 1st House. Where the key phrase for the 1st House is "I am," the key phrase here is "I have." Taurus is a fixed earth sign, and the resources necessary to sustain personal existence are drawn from the earth. The 2nd House is concerned with our ability to earn money in order to acquire material possessions, as well as how many and of what kind. In the natal chart, the sign on the 2nd House cusp (its ruler) and the planets positioned within the house itself, as well as any planets in Taurus, the position of Venus (the natural 2nd-House ruler), and any aspects to the 2nd-House planets, all contribute to determining how we acquire and utilize money and material resources. Because they form an integral part of the personality, the things of the 2nd House are often called "moveable resources." Wherever we go in life, we should be either able to take or obtain those things that are essential to our sustenance.

This is the second house of the first quadrant. The second house of the next quadrant, the 5th House, also indicates resources, but there it is the riches of the mother, family, clan, or heritage.

EXAMPLE

Marlon Brando's chart shows Capricorn on the 2nd House cusp. Here, the Sagittarian Ascendant adventurous nature is applied to ambitious, responsible, and practical dealings with money and its use for acquiring things that have lasting value. Mars located here indicates that his actions were focused on securing personal resources and that he probably had great physical endurance from an innate skill for expending his energy in due measure.

The 3rd House

 Sign: Gemini
Ruler: Mercury

Conscious thought and perception are the domain of the 3rd House, and here the key phrase is "I think." Gemini, the 3rd-House sign, is ruled by Mercury, making this the house concerned with assimilating, processing, and dispensing information. It is the house of the practical mind and the basic opportunities we are given to learn the essentials of communication and the exchange of ideas. It is also the house of brothers and sisters, childhood friends, neighbors, and so-called accidental or informal acquaintances. Having established identity in the 1st House, basic tools and resources in the 2nd, in the 3rd House we are now ready to receive new information and experiences that provide knowledge to be used in the future. Here, our native intellect is tested and communication skills developed. Every chance encounter provides an opportunity for this development to take place and build upon itself.

Any planets in Gemini, as well as the position of Mercury, provide additional insight into the 3rd House. The planets found in the 3rd House and along with the ruler of the sign appearing on the natal chart cusp, also help in determining the nature of the mentality at work and the primary experiences in learning and communicating.

EXAMPLE

Aquarius on Brando's 3rd-House cusp indicates he communicated his ideas in original, exciting, and often ingenious ways. His ideas would have come from flashes of intuition and insight which he was able to put to practical use, and his concerns were decidedly humanitarian in outlook. This house placement points to unusual and peculiar relationships with brothers, sisters, and neighbors.

Uranus appears to be located in Brando's 3rd House, but it is less than 2 degrees away from the 4th-House cusp and would therefore be considered to also have import in relation to 4th-House matters. When a planet is located within 3 to 6 degrees of an angular house cusp, it is referred to as an "angular planet" and has added influence in the natal chart.

The 4th House

Sign: Cancer
Ruler: The Moon

The second quadrant begins with the 4th House. Here are contained the things necessary for survival—family, shelter, and nourishment (the mother). It houses the basic currents of the personal unconscious, deeper sentiments, and the emotional attachments in which security is rooted, all of which are essentially hereditary.

The 4th House tells much about how and where we live, how we are affected by our immediate environment, and the kind of attachments we have to our tribe or nation, as well as our connections to our past and early childhood. The 4th House is strongly associated with early childhood, the beginning of life, that which forms and influences us, and with the end of life, when we are subject to the conditions we have ourselves created and, in effect, become like children again, dependent upon the care of others. It represents the final resting place of the physical body.

The 4th House rules homes, food, household items, and even mundane stuff like laundry—the kind of environment we create and maintain for ourselves, which can be a strong reflection of our mental and emotional makeup.

EXAMPLE

In Marlon Brando's natal chart, Pisces is on the cusp of the 4th House. With this position, the home is often a place of retreat, where privacy and seclusion are sought for introspection and meditation. Furthermore, Pisces' ruler, Neptune, is found in the 9th House, which has to do with foreign lands. Brando bought an island off Tahiti where he lived in seclusion for many years.

The Sun appears in Brando's 4th House. This is an indication that parental name, family affairs, and other domestic matters were of the utmost importance in his life.

The Sun brings honor, pride, and fame to anything under its influence. The problem of these influences here is that true success will probably not be attained until the mature years. This also indicates a very strong attachment to one of his parents, most likely his mother, which is further supported by the Moon also located in this house. He probably believed strongly in being the "ruler" in his home, and the sense of privacy would have been extensively developed in his nature.

The Moon in the 4th House probably influenced events concerning his mother, places of residence, and family matters. Both childhood and his later years were characterized by a love of romance, various journeys, and interesting adventures.

The liability of this astrological combination is that it can cause a perpetual striving for material security that seems to be hard to come by.

As mentioned in the previous section on the 3rd House, Uranus is located on the 4th-House cusp of Marlon's chart. Uranus, the planet of the erratic, unusual, and the freedom-loving, would seem to indicate there was upheaval in his childhood as well as in his domestic life later on. He probably had an unusual style of living and/or a home with all the latest conveniences.

The 5th House

 Sign: Leo
Ruler: The Sun

There is, we can see, a logical progression in the process of individuation as represented by the signs and the houses. In the 1st House, the self, identity, is established. In the 2nd, we see the resources gathered that enable the self to act; in the

3rd, the development of a mind to control and use those resources. In the 4th, a base of operations is established. In the 5th House, we are ready for creative self-expression and procreation.

This is the house of children, artistic creativity, dramatic self-assertion, love affairs, private enterprise, ethics and character, social entertainment, and recreation. In the 5th House, the Sun's dynamic power is expressed through the self, and in that sense it shows the way in which we love. Here, the joy of living is felt and expressed, and we desire to reach out and connect with that same life force in the one we love. From this union new progeny are born. In the 5th House, though, there is no true union of the sexes (this is found in the 7th and 8th Houses). It is more the house of courtship and romance in which we discover what we want in love and a lover and in which deference is shown to the one we are courting.

EXAMPLE

Brando's natal chart shows Aries on the cusp of the 5th House, suggesting that he brought much energy to creative activity and formulated many original concepts in that regard. In fact, it is often said that he changed the art of acting in the twentieth century, bringing his own method to the "Method," and influencing an entire generation of performers on stage and screen. Individuals with Aries on the 5th-House cusp are passionate and aggressive in love and romance. They love sports, especially those of a combative nature such as boxing, wrestling, and football. They are both dominating and generous in their relationships with children.

Mercury is located in the 5th House in Brando's chart. He had ample mental resources to contribute to successful self-expression and creative endeavors.

The 6th House

 Sign: Virgo
Ruler: Mercury

This is the house of work, of the labor necessary to bring to fruition that which was creatively envisioned in the 5th House. The planets in this house, the ruler of the house, and their aspects all reveal our attitude toward work, our methodology, and our ability to perform tasks and solve problems in a practical way. Here, discipline and training, with a comprehensive understanding combined with careful and patient attention to detail, are the skills that we must learn in order to handle these practical tasks and responsibilities. What is required here is a humble devotion to work and service. This is the house of the concerns and limits of the use of the practical mind for personal advantage. Here we learn the value of hard work, acquire new skills, observe the effect of our work and ideas on others, analyze and solve problems, and learn to be discriminating and thorough—all of which provide the practical security for the experiences defined in the houses still to follow: marriage, career, and social activity. In a sense, we have passed through spring and summer and are now entering autumn and preparing for the harvest.

The 6th House is also associated with health and hygiene, with the care and maintenance of the body as an essential instrument in the performance of duties and labors. It rules diet and cooking as well as clothing and appearance (cleanliness and neatness, or the lack thereof).

Any planets in Virgo will have an influence on the 6th House, and wherever they appear in the chart we must be realistic, analytical, hardworking, and thorough in every respect.

Whereas the 5th House relates to courtship and the 7th to marriage, the 6th House relates to betrothal or engagement. What we bring to any partnership at its inception is largely determined by the 6th House.

EXAMPLE

Taurus is on the cusp of the 6th House in Brando's chart. Although his work was practical and geared toward monetary gain (Taurus), it is enjoyed in projects that are artistic and beautiful (Venus, Taurus's ruler). His health tended to be generally robust, as long as the tendency to overeat or self-indulge in other ways was overcome.

Venus was in Brando's 6th House at the time of birth. He was definitely a lucky individual. His health throughout life was either very good or he was able to quickly recover from illness.

While he may have regarded his work as a pleasurable thing to do, he probably was not a hardworking individual; in fact, he probably exhibited a tendency toward laziness. Individuals with this Venus placement tend to find themselves in positions where they work under the direction of extremely benign and attractive superiors. A love relationship could start due to this interaction. As mentioned earlier, Brando's wives were all actresses, but he was also extremely fortunate in his professional training and his connections with great directors like Elia Kazan and Francis Ford Coppola.

In Brando's chart, notice that his Venus in Taurus is 5 degrees from the cusp of the 7th House, the Descendant, and can be considered angular. Therefore, Venus is very strong in his chart. As the ruler of Taurus and Libra, Venus is in dignity by sign and house, which is to say its energy flows very easily here, giving astrological testimony to Brando's physical attractiveness and palpable sensuality. Brando's commitment to his work and partnerships came very naturally to him.

• • •

The first six houses deal with the personal realms of life: the 1st with selfhood, the 2nd with acquisition, the 3rd with practical thought, the 4th with a personal base of operation, the 5th with creative self-expression, and the 6th with self-improvement through work and service. The last six houses deal with our relationships with other people and society as a whole, retracing, in a sense, the development of the first six houses and signs, but from a social reference point rather than a personal one.

The 7th House

 Sign: Libra
Ruler: Venus

One of the easiest ways to remember the symbolism of the houses is to look at the "self-other" axis represented by the houses opposite each other. Where the key phrase for the 1st House is "I am," that for the 7th is "We are." It represents the beginning of the objective, social phases of personal experience, where personal interests, aims, and desires are weighed and balanced against those of an "other." Formal agreements and contracts are made here, and we are concerned with all direct, close, personal relationships. The 7th House describes the kinds of partners we are likely to attract, in marriage and other close partnerships. The 7th House rules marriage, close friendships, public contacts, legal affairs, contracts, and agreements. It also governs commerce.

EXAMPLE

With Gemini on the 7th-House cusp, it's no surprise that Brando had more than one marriage and many significant partnerships, as the Sagittarian Ascendant shares with Gemini a tendency to have a wandering eye that is always looking for new and greener pastures. People with Gemini on the cusp of the 7th are primarily loners, but always manage to attract people of talent who can assist them in practical ways. Although astute and intelligent in public relations, they often prefer that their partners represent them and their ideas. When Brando was nominated Best Actor for his portrayal of Don Corleone in *The Godfather*, he sent a Native American woman to the Academy Award ceremony as his proxy; when the Oscar was awarded to him, she carried out his instruction to announce his denial of the award in protest against the U.S. government's infringement of Native American territorial rights.

The 8th House

 Sign: Scorpio
Rulers: Mars and Pluto

This is the house of joint resources, as its opposite, the 2nd House, is the house of personal property. The key phrase here is "We have." In some ways, it is perhaps the most difficult of the houses to understand. It deals with such diverse matters as sexuality, death, partnerships in terms of the sharing of assets, taxes, and psychic or extrasensory perceptions. In occult tradition, it is known as the house of spiritual transformation. The death symbolized in the 8th House can be seen as the death of selfishness or an ego-death. Here we have the capacity to pass through the purgatory of selfhood to the threshold of an understanding and appreciation of the more spiritual and universal aspects of life, and we are better able to understand the needs, desires, and beliefs of our mate or partner. In the 7th House, we are faced with the challenge to learn the balance of give and take that enables a suitable agreement with the other party. In the 8th House, a serious catharsis of egotistical attachments may take place as a natural progression of how we deal with our 7th-House issues.

In a successful marriage (the 7th House), the union finds its deepest expression in the 8th House, the house of shared resources. The treasures of the partner become our own, and vice versa. This finds one of its most profound expressions in the realm of sex. On the negative side, the baser desires of the 8th-House rulers, Mars and Scorpio, can be a source of conflict over jointly held wealth.

The 8th House is concerned with the death of the physical body and the practical matters associated with it—funerals, wills, and inheritance. It is also concerned with internal mystical experiences, the occult, and such aspects of science as higher mathematics and nuclear physics.

EXAMPLE

Marlon Brando's natal chart shows Cancer on the 8th-House cusp. With this position, the Sagittarian Ascendant becomes intensely emotional regarding his own death, and it is of utmost importance to him that he be remembered well and fondly after having passed on and that he leave behind ample provisions for those in his care.

The importance of 8th-House issues in Brando's life is further emphasized by Pluto in Cancer in the 8th House. Pluto here is in accidental dignity, being found in the house it naturally rules. It is likely that his partnerships exerted a profound transformation on his inner self, and he may have been at times either the dominating partner or at the mercy of his partner's demands, which would have involved Cancer concerns of motherhood, nurturing, emotional fulfillment, and the home.

The 9th House

 Sign: Sagittarius
Rulers: Jupiter and Neptune

The key phrase for the 9th House is "We think" (as opposed to the "I think" of the 3rd House). This house deals with philosophy, religion, and religious institutions, laws and legal systems, and institutions of higher learning—all those arenas in which social concepts are developed, embodied, and taught. It is related to teaching and publishing (through which knowledge is passed on to succeeding generations) and to long-distance travel, especially to foreign countries (through which greater personal knowledge of culture and humanity is gained). It is the house of idealism, education, social enlightenment, and conscience. It is concerned with truth and expansion. Here, the creative impulses and experiences of the 1st and 5th Houses are given added depth and breadth by combining with the experience, knowledge, and intuitive insights of others. This is the beginning of the attainment of the international or cosmopolitan worldview symbolized by the 10th, 11th, and 12th Houses.

EXAMPLE

Brando's chart shows Leo on the 9th-House cusp. Although these individuals may *appear* to not desire fame, they are subconsciously and philosophically geared toward attaining positions of importance in their particular fields of endeavor. Their eyes are constantly on large and distant goals, and they take many long journeys, both physically and mentally.

Neptune appears in the 9th House in Brando's chart. This diffuse energy would have contributed to an unusual education and a kind of mystical sense of how to apply his intellectual abilities. Neptune's strong artistic energy here in the 9th-House realm of mass communication fits well with his success as an actor who has become a cultural icon.

The 10th House

 Sign: Capricorn
Ruler: Saturn

Whereas the 4th House deals with our personal base of operations, the 10th House represents our social base and is concerned with such things as profession, career, political and business power structures, and public reputation and honor (or dishonor). The planets within this house, their aspects, the ruler of the house, and the sign placed within it all determine the nature of our ambition, how it will be manifested, and our ability to attain power or significance in the world. It shows how we will be favored or maligned by those in authority, the kind of employers we are likely to have, and our relationship to them.

The cusp of the 10th House, the Midheaven, can represent our zenith, both materially and spiritually, but only if we have managed to rise to its challenge.

EXAMPLE

With Virgo on the 10th-House cusp, the indication is that Brando was very particular about his public image. In professional roles, people with Virgo in the 10th House can appear efficient, organized, and circumspect, and often critical, cold, and aloof. In his later years, Brando expressed his disdain for his profession as an actor, calling it shallow and meaningless.

The 11th House

 Sign: Aquarius
Rulers: Uranus and Saturn

The 11th House is associated with creative group expression, with objective and impersonal truths rather than personal ones (as represented by the 5th House, its opposite). It is associated with embracing new ideas and experiences, freedom of expression, and a sense of shared loyalty and mutual responsibility. It reveals our capacity to make friends, communicate, form group associations, and understand and act from the standpoint of social and universal concerns. Here, we attain significance and fulfillment through our alliance with a group where ideals are shared and acted upon in the name of some humanitarian endeavor.

This is the house in which we make friendships in the name of higher purposes and shared ideals rather than personal advantage or gratification. The intellect, rather than the emotions, is the driving force here, and of primary concern is the view toward the future. Although the family is far from forgotten, it is here that community or society counts the most, and the overall betterment of everyone in it. Open relationships are favored, especially those that are based on socially important aims and ideals.

Any planets in Aquarius and the position of Uranus in the chart influence the power of the 11th House.

EXAMPLE

Libra is on the cusp of Brando's 11th House. Individuals with a Libra 11th House often obtain their goals by surrounding themselves with artistic, attractive, and unusual friends who are prosperous and stable. Often, they marry a friend or a friend of a friend.

Saturn was in the 11th House at the time of Brando's birth. Psychologically, this can indicate a hidden and limited view of personal ambitions, friendships, and the future. He may have been ambitious, cautious, just, patient, responsible, but at times too serious. He probably had few friends, and even these people may have been more inclined to offer assistance when it was needed in the form of advice rather than with actual help.

The 12th House

 Sign: Pisces
Rulers: Neptune and Jupiter

As the house corresponding with the water sign Pisces, the 12th House is believed to contain the seeds of the next incarnation as revealed by the 1st House. This is the house of personal secrets, self-judgment, karma, solitude, memory, meditation, universal understanding, and compassion. Both great joy and great sorrow can be found in the 12th House.

It is the final house of the horoscopic wheel and reveals
how great deeds (the 10th House) and altruistic concerns (the
11th House) can be incorporated into a broad, compassionate,
and penetrating intelligence, one imbued with a sense of life's
unity and mystery. Contemplative solitude, intuitive understanding, and self-sacrifice all arise from the 12th House.

Here, too, are all the unresolved karmic issues. The 12th
House, like the 8th House, can be difficult to understand.
Residing in it are both hidden support and self-undoing.
Success or failure at the earlier stages of life (and perhaps past
lives) is reckoned in the 12th House. Here, the ghosts of the
past can come to haunt us. All things considered subversive or
evil are also found in this house—psychosis, imprisonment,
sorrow, destitution, loneliness, bondage, perversity. The criminal, liar, drug addict, deviant, spy, alcoholic, and wastrel are
subject to Neptune's influence. But it is here, too, where acts
of good will and charity are performed, and even enlightenment attained.

EXAMPLE

Scorpio is on the cusp of Brando's 12th House. Here, his
Sagittarian Ascendant manifests a hidden resourcefulness that
is often not immediately apparent to others. He was able to
recognize things of value that others overlooked or failed to
perceive—that which was "hidden in plain sight." He also
knew how to cultivate and bring out the hidden talents of others. Secret love affairs and hidden resentments probably
caused him a great deal of strife.

CHAPTER 4

THE MAJOR ASPECTS:
CONJUNCTIONS, SEXTILES, SQUARES, TRINES, AND OPPOSITIONS

Y ou have learned about the signs, planets, and houses. These fundamental elements of the chart tell you about the available energy and where it tends to come into play, but aspects tell you about how planets work together in the chart, the manner in which their energies are blended, and how they tend to get used.

An aspect is the angle formed between two imaginary lines connecting two celestial bodies or points (such as the Ascendant or Midheaven) to the Earth. There are several kinds of aspects that planets can form, but focusing on the five major aspects will give you plenty to work with in the beginning of your astrological study. The major aspects are the conjunction (0 degrees), sextile (60 degrees), square (90 degrees), trine (120 degrees), and opposition (180 degrees). Among these aspects, the squares and oppositions are considered to be challenging, while the conjunctions, trines, and sextiles are considered harmonious, but this depends on the planets involved. The minor aspects are the inconjunct or quincunx (150 degrees), semi-sextile (30 degrees), semisquare (45 degrees), sesquisquare (135 degrees), quintile (72 degrees), and the biquintile (144 degrees).

ORB OF INFLUENCE

Planets don't have to be exactly at a particular degree from each other to be considered as forming aspects to one another. The effect of an aspect begins to be felt as the planets draw nearer the exact degree of the aspect. If they fall within a certain range of the exact aspect degree, they are in aspect. This range is known as the orb of influence and can be thought of as a kind of "gravitational pull." Some astrologers work with a tight orb of 5 to 6 degrees for the sextile and a wider orb of 10 degrees for the other major aspects, particularly when the luminaries (Sun and Moon) are involved.

For example, if Mars is at 15 degrees Taurus, an exact square to another planet would be 15 degrees Aquarius (or Leo—about three signs away in either direction around the wheel). With a 10-degree orb, any planet from 5 (15 minus 10) degrees Aquarius to 25 (15 plus 10) degrees Aquarius would be considered as forming a square with Mars. Where this gets tricky is when the planet is over 20 or under 10 degrees into a sign, as a sign occupies 30 degrees of the horoscopic wheel. So with a 22-degree Mars in Taurus, a planet between 12 (22 minus 10) degrees Aquarius and 2 degrees Pisces (22 plus 10 equals 32 degrees, minus 30 degrees equals 2 degrees into the next sign) forms a square to Mars. On the other end of the arc, with Mars at 3 degrees Taurus, any planet between 23 (3 minus 10 equals -7 plus 30 equals 23 degrees in the sign preceding) degrees Capricorn and 13 (3 plus 10) degrees Aquarius would be forming a square to Mars. All of this will become more clear as you learn about each aspect described in the following section.

THE CONJUNCTION
♂

A conjunction is the occurrence of a direct or nearly direct lineup of two planets as seen from the Earth (see figure 7 on page 82). These are planets in the same sign, 5 (for the outer planets) to 10 (for the inner planets) degrees apart. Key phrases here are "has an affinity with," "likeness to," "shares an experience," "identifies in purpose with," "of a similar nature." In Marlon Brando's chart, his Sun and Moon are one degree apart in Aries and are therefore conjunct. His conscious, fundamental essence and will (Sun) worked in concert with his emotional needs and intuition (Moon).

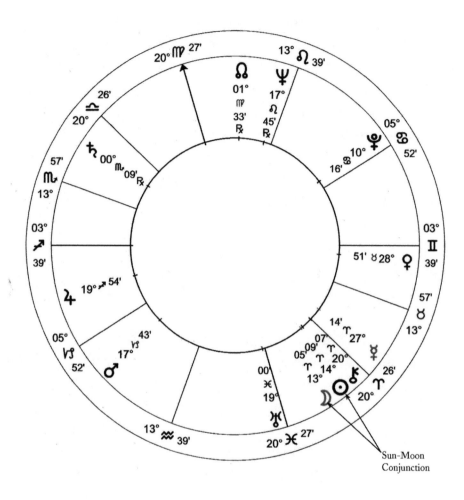

Sun-Moon
Conjunction

*Fig. 7. Conjunction of Sun and Moon in
Marlon Brando's natal chart.*

THE SEXTILE
✳

This aspect represents an angular relationship of 60 degrees, or one-sixth of a circle. Planets in sextile are placed two signs apart and occupy approximately the same number of degrees in these signs, plus or minus 6 degrees.

Key phrases for planets in sextile are "stimulates or accentuates," "connects favorable with or relates to," "communicates sympathy for," "furthers the purpose or interest of," "helps reveal a side of." See figure 8 below.

In figure 9 on page 84, Marlon Brando's chart shows Mars in Capricorn sextile Uranus in Pisces.

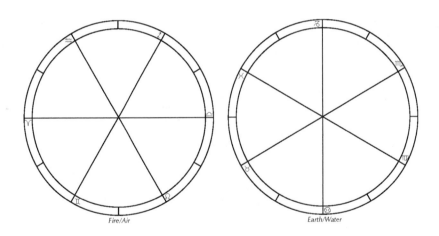

Fig. 8. Sextiles.

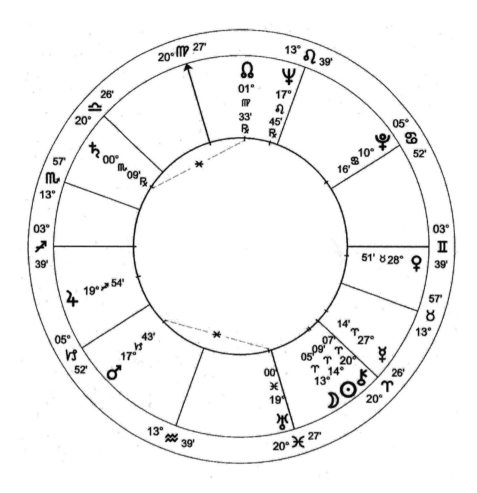

Fig. 9. Mars in Capricorn sextile Uranus in Pisces in Brando's natal chart.

THE SQUARE
□

A square represents an angular relationship of 90 degrees between two planets. Planets in square generally occupy the same number of degrees in signs which are three signs apart. Key phrases here are "in conflict with," "excited or activated by," "demands or requires an adjustment between," "problems between." The planets involved in the square determine whether the energy will be activating or of a conflicting nature. See figure 10.

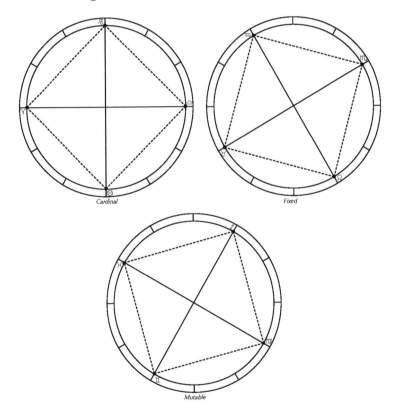

Fig. 10. Squares and oppositions.

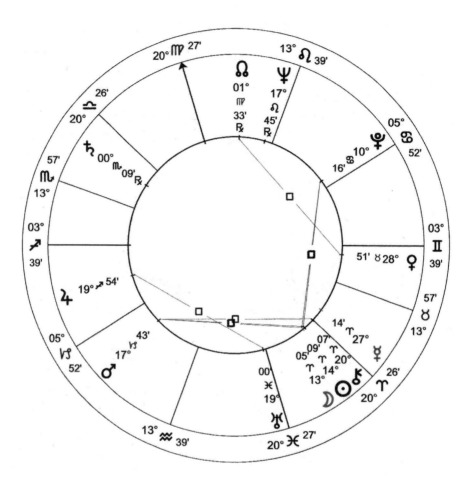

Fig. 11. Squares in Brando's natal chart.

Brando's chart has several squares due to his Sun-Moon conjunction—Sun square Mars, Sun square Pluto, Moon square Mars and Moon square Pluto—and Jupiter square Uranus. See figure 11.

THE TRINE
△

A trine is an angular relationship of 120 degrees or one-third of a circle between two planets. Planets in trine generally occupy the same number of degrees in signs four signs apart. Key phrases here are "blends well or harmonizes with," "favors one another," "supports," "positively mirrors," "aids in fulfillment," "of a similar nature," "shares common interest," "joins in the expression of." See figure 12.

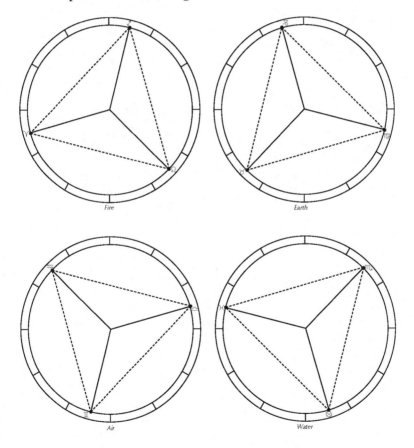

Fig. 12. Trines.

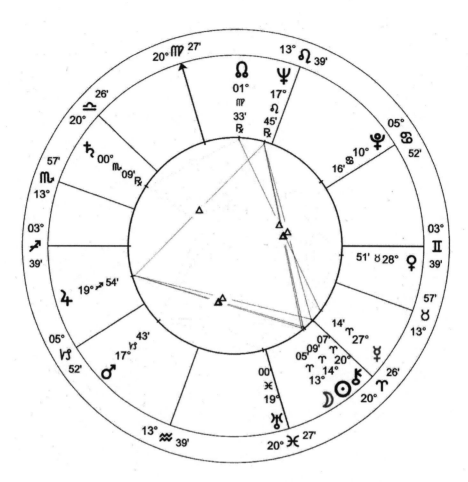

Fig. 13. Trines in Brando's natal chart. Note the Sun–Moon in Aries conjunction in a grand trine with Jupiter in Sagittarius and Neptune in Leo.

Figure 13 shows several trines, including a grand fire trine (three planets within 120 degrees of each other in each sign of an element) in Marlon Brando's natal chart.

THE OPPOSITION
☍

An opposition is an angular relationship of 180 degrees between two planets (see figure 10, page 85). Planets in opposition generally occupy approximately the same number of degrees in two signs directly across the Zodiac from each other. Key phrases here are "antagonizes," "agitates," "counters," "requires adjustment to," "complements," "collides or clashes with," "demands compromise between," "affects profoundly," "dramatically unites," "out of harmony with." Brando's natal chart contains an opposition between Mercury in Aries and Saturn in Scorpio. See figure 14 on page 90.

Also in Brando's chart, Venus is in opposition to his Ascendant, indicating that he was drawn to refined and sophisticated people. This aspect indicates he himself was well mannered, and generally people had a good opinion of him. He would have been inclined to make concessions if they appeared necessary to maintain harmonious relations. Although he appeared self-confident and assured, it was probably difficult for him to stand alone. He worked hard, although subtly, to hide his deep insecurities. His friends were probably his best PR agents, freely and enthusiastically extolling his virtues.

On the surface, individuals with Venus in opposition to the Ascendant appear as docile, gentle, and charming (Venus), but underneath they tend to conspire and scheme to advance and better themselves (Ascendant) through the people they deal with; this is the 1st-House/7th-House axis dynamic in action.

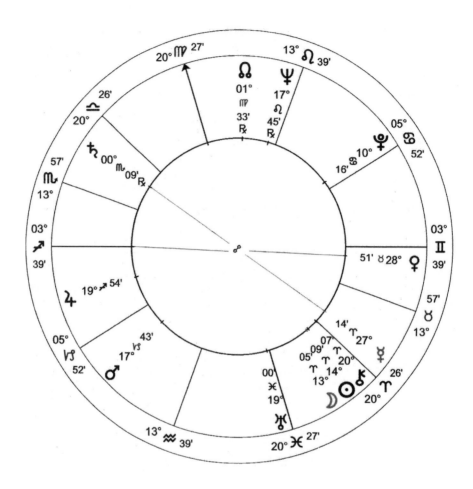

Fig. 14. Mercury in Aries opposition to Saturn in Scorpio in Brando's natal chart; Venus in the late degrees of Taurus opposes his Ascendant in the early degrees of Sagittarius as well.

PART 2

THE PLANETS IN THE SIGNS, HOUSES, AND ASPECT

CHAPTER 5

THE SUN

T he Sun represents our vital force, conscious purpose, and essential character. It is associated with the masculine yang principle and consciousness.

THE SUN IN THE SIGNS

Reading the following descriptions of the twelve signs, you should bear in mind that they apply not only to the Sun sign, which denotes will and purpose, but also to the Rising Sign, which denotes personality and attitudes.

Sun in Aries—March 21 to April 20

I am.

Symbol: The Ram
Planetary Ruler: Mars
Element: Fire
Quality: Cardinal
Complementary Sign: Libra

Aries represents the birth of individual will, and as a result, persons born under this sign tend to be characterized by their initiative, fortitude, courage, virtuosity, curiosity, and originality. They tend to be warm and energetic, full of inspiration and incentive, with pronounced qualities of leadership and self-reliance. Here, too, we can perceive competitiveness, impulsiveness, lack of restraint, combativeness, self-centeredness, and narcissism.

Aries, the Ram, meets obstacles head-on, overcomes them, and moves on to explore new horizons. It is the sign of challenge and conquest. Arians base their actions on their strong intuitive sense and belief in themselves. They can be highly persuasive, but it is often necessary for them to develop tact, reserve, thoroughness, and receptivity to others in order to avoid the pitfalls of excessive self-confidence, forcefulness, and a lack of subtlety or diplomacy in their dealings with others. At the same time, more than any other sign, Arians must know how to take immediate and individual action in dealing with the personal crises they are bound to encounter.

In love, Aries wants foremost to be admired by his or her lover or mate. Some Aries individuals see love in terms of conquest and their ardent need for self-actualization through both the lover and any children that result from the union.

Aries rules the head and face, eyes, brain, ears, nose, upper jaw, and the pituitary and pineal glands.

Sun in Taurus—April 21 to May 21

I have.
Symbol: The Bull
Planetary Ruler: Venus
Element: Earth
Quality: Fixed
Complementary Sign: Scorpio

Taurus is the sign of the builder and the cultivator of crops, characterized by the practical utilization of the resources at hand. Consistency and thoroughness and ensuring that seeds are gathered for future planting are hallmarks of this sign in its most positive manifestations—hallmarks that are, in fact, essential to its nature and purpose. With steadfastness, perseverance, and an eye for the small but important details, Taurians are able to build that which endures and provides personal security and contentment. On the other hand, it is of vital strategic importance that those born under this fixed sign not jeopardize themselves by exhausting their personal resources, a situation that can prove to be especially dangerous to Taurus.

A common pitfall among Taurians can be a tendency to be overly concerned with the mundane and material world and to adopt a point of view that lacks flexibility and ignores the rewards of experience beyond the purely practical. A narrow-minded selfishness and concern for material gain can be evident in the less developed of this sign, who can also exhibit a lack of emotional sensitivity and a distinct lack of humor when it comes to themselves. They can be stubborn, dull, excessively conservative, impatient, and procrastinating. On the positive side, they are gifted with down-to-earth common sense, stamina, patience, and the ability to construct solid foundations and accumulate wealth.

Taurus is concerned with the practical aspects of marriage and the comforts and rewards it can provide that are constructive and supportive in increasing personal productivity.

Taurus rules the lower jaw, tongue, uvula, tonsils, throat and neck, pharynx, epiglottis, larynx, trachea, Eustachian tube, and the thyroid and parathyroid glands.

Sun in Gemini—May 22 to June 21

I think.

Symbol: The Twins
Planetary Ruler: Mercury
Element: Air
Quality: Mutable
Complementary Sign: Sagittarius

Gemini is the sign of communication and its various forms, the logical third step after Aries (self and will) and Taurus (the builder of the material foundations on which the self can endure). Persons born under this sign are excellent translators and conveyors of information, with the ability to consider two points of view at once. Geminis are highly adaptable and versatile, and their bipolar intellect can sometimes make them highly changeable, which explains Gemini's symbol of the twins.

The position of Mercury in a Gemini's chart is especially important, as Mercury's position in the horoscope shows the particular outlet for intellectual energy, and Mercury is never more than 28 degrees away from the Sun. Therefore, there can only be three types of Gemini or Gemini mentality: Gemini, Taurian, and Cancerian. Along with the house position of the Sun, Mercury's position shows how the Gemini correlates information and then communicates it.

When negative, Geminis can be superficial and verbose, plagiaristic, inconsistent, and mercurial. The Gemini must develop a sense of pragmatism and self-confidence to succeed. This sign is at its best when it remains open, objective, and adaptable and uses its considerable talents of interpretation and communication to informally teach others.

In love, Gemini seeks communication and stimulating companionship. In some ways, this individual looks for a mate who is more like a brother or sister, searching for a "twin" or counterpart, who is also flexible and adaptable.

Gemini rules the bronchi and lungs, collarbone, shoulders, arms, hands, upper ribs, and nerves.

Sun in Cancer—June 22 to July 23

I feel.
Symbol: The Crab
Planetary Ruler: The Moon
Element: Water
Quality: Cardinal
Complementary Sign: Capricorn

Words directly associated with Cancer are the mother, the family, the home, nourishment, security, and protection. Cancer people are naturally skilled at acquiring the essentials of life, but these essentials can sometimes become confused with things that have inherently personal or sentimental value; hence their homes can appear cluttered with nonessentials. This exaggerated or neurotic need for security is a result of a distortion of the feminine instincts, as Cancer is the most feminine and maternal of all the signs. Even Cancer men exhibit strong feminine characteristics—both positive and negative—under their often tough and burly exteriors. In this regard, the Cancer woman is of singular interest as a manifestation of the archetypal female.

There are two kinds of Cancer woman—the mother or the eternal girl, *puella eterna*; sometimes she is a mixture of both. Cancer is the epitome of enigmatic femaleness. Alluring and elusive, she is intuitive, instinctive, ruled by the Moon and the shifting tides of her moods. She is unpredictable, alternately loving and cruel, shrewd yet innocent and childlike, capable of surprising ruthlessness, driving ambition, and ultimately full of mystery. The maternal, domestic aspect of Cancer heals, nurtures, and supports. Her other aspect is wild, fierce, strong, full of emotional tempests, unforgiving, and essentially primitive, sometimes even perverse, like Mother Nature herself. This dark, primal, and archaic aspect of the Goddess fascinates, attracts, frightens, and repels.

Positive Cancer people all show a desire and capacity to nurture and protect others in some way. They have great powers of empathy and are likely to be champions of the underdog. They rely strongly on their feelings and impressions, which can be taken too far, making them overly subjective and lacking a realistic view of the matter or individual at hand. In its negative mode, Cancer can be insular, defensive, clinging, self-indulgent, chauvinistic, manipulative, slothful, and overly emotional and sentimental.

Cancer is a sign associated with the personal unconscious, especially as it is affected and formed by early childhood and environment. It is highly receptive to the impressions that arise from these deeper levels of consciousness and therefore can be prone to have a highly creative imagination.

In a mate or partner, Cancer looks for nourishment, empathy, and security. There is a need for a companion who is tolerant of Cancer's moods and tendency to collect and store things.

Cancer rules the breasts, mammary glands, armpits, upper abdominal cavity, esophagus, stomach, pancreas, and uterus.

Sun in Leo—July 24 to August 23

I will.

Symbol: The Lion
Planetary Ruler: The Sun
Element: Fire
Quality: Fixed
Complementary Sign: Aquarius

Leo is the sign of creative self-expression and enterprise. Leo sets an example for others and gives them direction. Creation, recreation, and procreation are the three terms that describe the leonine purpose. Positive Leos promote the joy of being and a sense of justice and ethics in dealing with others. This is especially true in regard to their children. As lions, or lionesses, they have an acute and dignified sense of both the individual and the lion pride, that is, the family or group, and how the two work together and nurture each other. Leos are magnetic, warm, and outgoing individuals, gentle but firm, exuberant and bold, making them the epitome of the archetypal king or queen. The symbol of this sign is the lion, denoting majesty, power, and dignity. As Shakespeare has Henry V describe his ideal of himself as he walks in disguise among his troops on the eve of battle—"For forth he goes, a largesse, universal like the sun, his liberal eye doth give to everyone"—so is the point and satisfaction of being for a Leo.

Leos are strongly attracted to the opposite sex. It is often necessary for the passionate and dramatic nature of leonine love to be held in check, as heartache can be the result. The French as a nation are ruled by Leo.

Egocentricity, personal aggrandizement, insincerity, and domineering or manipulative behavior can be evident when Leo is in its negative mode. They can be pompous, bombastic, excessively dramatic, and show a pronounced lack of self-restraint. They can become sullen, brooding, and petulant when slighted or things do not conform to their desires. If their fire is squelched, they can be like the cowardly lion in the *Wizard of Oz*, acutely lacking in self-esteem and overly subservient and conformist to the ideas and conventions around them, while compensating with a ridiculous and empty show of pomposity, vanity, and personal adornment.

An almost childlike spontaneity, playfulness, and a sense of humor are positive and delightful expressions of the Leo personality. They are able to invigorate and entertain others and inspire them to action under their benevolent and charismatic leadership. Both Napoleon and T. E. Lawrence (Lawrence of Arabia) are wonderful examples of a Leo in both its positive and negative expressions.

The poetic idea of the lion heart, the *coeur du lion*, is equated in English and French Medieval literature to a benign and noble sense of both the self and others under which all individuals flourish—the Sun in its rulership of the planets that revolve around it. Call it love as the primary principle and motive—Leo's inner guiding light. The writer Iris Murdoch has written that, "Love is the perception of individuals . . . the extremely difficult realization that something other than oneself is real." It is the freedom from "the proliferation of blinding self-centered aims and images . . . that is the realism of compassion."

This principle is essential to Leo consciousness. Leo rules the heart and is the sign of generosity and nobility of feeling. When the source of Leo's power comes from deep in the heart and is freely expressed and demonstrated, the greater its influence is felt. When this light is darkened, and heart and benevolence are lacking, the Lion can take on the grim characteristics of a petulant, cruel, and petty tyrant. But in its most positive and radiant manifestation, the dispensing of good will, fairness, and most importantly, joy is an almost religious principle for those born under the sign of Leo.

Leos seek a willing audience in their partners with whom they can share their plans and designs. Some may simply want a playmate. Women born under this sign tend to dominate their marriages and will be like ferocious lionesses when it comes to defending their children. Children are an important part of marriage for many born under the sign of the Lion.

Leo rules the heart and aorta, the back, spinal cord and column, and the thymus.

Sun in Virgo—August 24 to September 23

I analyze.

Symbol: The Virgin
Planetary Ruler: Mercury
Element: Earth
Quality: Mutable
Complementary Sign: Pisces

Owing to its mutability, Virgo is considerably more adaptable and mobile than Taurus, a fixed sign and the first of the earth signs. It is associated with observation, critical analysis, practical application, craftsmanship, service and assistance, instruction (the "how to," rather than the theory), and rules and doctrine. Virgos seek simplicity, pragmatism, and precision in their lives. Their task is the prevention of disorder and the maintenance and repair of all the individual parts of an organic whole. Their analytical skills make them highly suited to any job requiring sedulous attention to practical details. It is this discriminating and orderly sign that ensures the bountiful and usable crop sown by Taurus.

When negative, Virgos can be obsessive about unnecessary details and neurotic about order and hygiene. They can show a marked lack of warmth and sympathy for those who do not conform to their standards and be overly critical and analytical to the detriment of their personal and social relationships.

A Virgo's role is to serve; it is that of the mechanic or engineer who quietly ensures that the machine keeps running. The Virgo should, however, be supremely aware of the value of his or her skills and craftsmanship and not enslave or prostitute them in the service of others.

In love and marriage, Virgos seek a working relationship in which order and common sense enable both parties to establish a smoothly running relationship. Some Virgos are more than happy to serve the aims of their partner.

Virgo rules the upper intestines and the spleen.

Sun in Libra—September 24 to October 23

I balance.

Symbol: The Scales
Planetary Ruler: Venus
Element: Air
Quality: Cardinal
Complementary Sign: Aries

Libra is the sign primarily concerned with relationships, marriage, partnerships, and cooperation, of the harmonious balance between self and other. The first air sign, Gemini, symbolized by the Twins, represents accidental or informal relationships, while Libra represents relationships that are more formal and contractual in nature, and in which roles, duties, and commitments are clearly proscribed.

Arbitration, justice, reason, comparison, mediation, negotiation, and agreement are words associated with this sign. Positive Librans exhibit an inherent detachment and ability to weigh, balance, and reasonably assess the merits of a situation. Libra is also associated with art and beauty, especially in terms of form and design. Librans seek harmonious unions with others to find the complement to their own qualities that will ensure and enhance their success. Cooperation, especially with a mate or partner, is of the utmost importance to them.

A typical pitfall of Libra in its negative mode can be indecisiveness and timidity brought on by its tendency to endlessly weigh things and to be fearful of others' disapproval. When Librans are capable of acting decisively after carefully weighing things properly, they become potential leaders and counselors able to solve problems and end disputes and conflicts.

The kind of alliances a Libra forms determine the kind of rewards he or she will reap. With their special need for union and companionship and strong concern for peace and harmony, it is of vital importance that Librans maintain a sense of their individuality in their relationships with others.

Venus imbues Libra with charm, sensuality, and graceful self-expression, along with a strong desire for popularity. However, positive Librans will never compromise their principles to gain approval, as they are as equally aware of humiliation as they are approbation. As an air sign, they are prone to be intellectuals and active seekers of knowledge. All matters pertaining to human relationships and psychology are of vital interest to them, and they are especially adept at analyzing what is occurring in the society around them.

In a relationship or marriage, Libra seeks mutual appreciation and commitment. Cooperation is the basic aim toward which Libra directs its energies. Tactful and graceful concern for the partner needs to be balanced with respect for the Libran's own personal aims and concerns.

Libra rules the lower abdominal cavity, the lumbar, lower ribs, kidneys, ureters, adrenal glands, ovaries, and oviducts.

Sun in Scorpio–October 24 to November 22

I desire.

Symbol: The Scorpion
Planetary Rulers: Mars and Pluto
Element: Water
Quality: Fixed
Complementary Sign: Taurus

Scorpio is the sign concerned with the sharing of wealth and resources, both physically and mentally. As the eighth sign directly following Libra, Scorpio's primary concern should be the proper alignment of its talents and resources with those it is in communion with. It is, in its positive manifestation, the sign that enriches others. When Scorpio shares what it possesses with its partner, it is itself enriched.

More than any other sign, Scorpio deals with the processes of transformation and self-renewal, which can be manifested on a high or low level, depending on motivation. This sign is strongly driven by desire, including sex, and there is great emotional force behind all of its attachments. As a result, when negative, Scorpio can be possessive and jealous, and its vengeance can be lethal if it is crossed or scorned.

Like Cancer and Pisces—the other water signs—Scorpio is inclined to be covert and secretive, intuitively connected to life's mysteries and relying on its psychic powers and feelings. Indeed, Scorpios can be highly psychic without being aware of it, a power that can be dangerous or destructive when misdirected or not properly applied. To Scorpio, a fixed water sign, life can be seen as a glacier that one has to cross, avoiding the many emotional and sensual crevasses that present themselves along the way. A struggle with the passions can be, for Scorpio, a prelude to self-transformation and renewal. However, being a sign of will and desire, it is easy for the lower type to use its personal magnetism, astute insight, and hypnotic powers to gain personal advantage, which is the last thing a Scorpio should be concerned about.

The eagle, the highest manifestation of the Scorpio principle, uses its penetrating intelligence to regenerate and heal life's defects. This can be especially true in relationships, in which Scorpios can be instrumental in alleviating the emotional and/or sexual problems of their partners. This is the sign associated with the surgeon, the biologist, the scientist, the depth psychologist, and others who study and comprehend the forces of life and death. They are compelled to investigate the hidden nature of things, and as a result tend to excel in work involving detection, research, science, and the occult. When spiritually developed, they derive great power from their innate abilities to tap into life's fundamental creative and regenerative forces.

Scorpios never deal with life superficially, and no other sign has such a potent capacity for good or evil. Unlike Aries, the other sign ruled by Mars and Pluto, they have tremendous staying power (being a fixed sign) and will see any matter through to the bitter end, regardless of the effort and sacrifice required.

Physically, they tend to be robust and often possess hypnotically penetrating eyes and an alluring mystique (think of Picasso, in many ways a typical Scorpio).

Romantically, Scorpio seeks sexual union and fulfillment along with an equitable sharing of resources.

Scorpio rules the lower intestines, rectum, anus, sacral and pubic areas, buttocks, bladder, urethra, genitals, appendix, and sweat glands.

Sun in Sagittarius—November 23 to December 21

I see.

Symbol: The Archer
Planetary Ruler: Jupiter
Element: Fire
Quality: Mutable
Complementary Sign: Gemini

Truth and a deep love of liberty and freedom are, in many ways, the primary concerns of Sagittarius, the third of the fire signs. A high-minded idealism, frankness, swift yet precise judgment, and boldness of action are characteristic of those born under the sign of the Archer. Here is the serious philosophical thinker, concerned with ideas and the overall well-being of society and the ethics and laws that govern it. They are at home with abstract thoughts and concepts and possess a deep yearning for knowledge and experience. They are honest, generous, gregarious, and just, concerned with the approval and harmony of the society in which they live.

Idealism is a hallmark of Sagittarius, but this same zeal can become religious or political fanaticism or a blind adherence to dogmas and laws. They can become narrow-minded and bigoted according to the biases of the social and moral standards to which they subscribe. In these cases, it is vital that the Sagittarian evolve mentally beyond such limitations and embrace more expansive concepts.

Sagittarians have an uncanny ability to see the future based on their perceptions of the current trends and events around them. Their visceral desire for knowledge and experience makes them highly adventurous, both mentally and physically, and in both realms they will travel far and wide.

The swiftness and accuracy of the Archer can also make them impulsive and prone to jump to conclusions without considering all the factors involved. Sagittarians who shoot at their targets without the required discipline and skill can become hopelessly lost in the forest in which they hunt. They do, however, always speak the truth as to how they see it, and they can be unmerciful in dealing with their enemies.

For some, it may be necessary to develop a sense of logic to go along with their ideals, expansive enthusiasm, and grandiose plans. Overconfidence and excessive zeal can lead to taking reckless chances and making hasty judgments. The more knowledge and understanding the Sagittarian can acquire, the more he or she is able to accomplish.

The sharing of an ideal or idea, along with a spirit of mental and physical adventure that more often than not involves the willingness to travel, is at the heart of what Sagittarius seeks in a mate.

Sagittarius rules the thighs, hips, liver, and gall bladder.

Sun in Capricorn–December 22 to January 20

I use.

Symbol: The Goat
Planetary Ruler: Saturn
Element: Earth
Quality: Cardinal
Complementary Sign: Cancer

At its best, Capricorn symbolizes the paternal side of human nature, as Cancer, its complementary opposite, represents the maternal. Capricorn looks to the future based on the past, learning from humanity's mistakes as well as its achievements, and is thus able to use and capitalize on things of quality and worth. In its quest for excellence and recognition, no task or detail is too tedious or mundane for the sure-footed goat as it cautiously makes it way along the perilous trails leading to the mountain heights. Carelessness, lack of order, and ill-defined duties and goals can bring about the downfall of those driven by Saturn's ambition.

Having great faith in their own power, and with their practical knowledge and capacity for hard work, they are never deterred by any obstacles that stand in their way and are extremely adept at finding solutions to difficult problems. In fact, just being a Capricorn means that there are obstacles or barriers that must be overcome or burdens to be carried. They are born with the ability to utilize everything they see, hear, or learn. For Capricorn, success means material security, and they will strive relentlessly to achieve it. Capricorns tend to be old when they are young, and young when they are old, making them long-lived and thus desirous of acquiring power and money as a way to forestall being dependent on anyone.

Although they will inevitably find themselves in a position of authority or power, Capricorns are always aware there is a higher authority to which they must answer. They are extremely conscious of the chain of command in their climb to the top. In outlook and attitude, they are basically traditional and conservative.

Besides giving in to ruthless ambition, negative Capricorns can harbor dark fears of hidden enemies and have overly stern, serious, and taciturn natures, which can, in fact, cause mistrust and resentment in those around them, thus creating a self-fulfilling prophesy. Melancholic brooding and brusqueness can also deprecate this sign in the eyes of others, especially subordinates.

Positive Capricorns, on the other hand, have great executive abilities and are able to dexterously handle any criticism, controversy, responsibility, or competition they may encounter. At its highest evolution, this is the most public of signs, and the best way for the Capricorn to achieve his or her goals is by maintaining integrity and clarity in all dealings.

In marriage, the Capricorn primarily seeks stability and a partner who can further, in some way, his or her career or social status. The partner must also be capable of accepting responsibility and making his or her own way. Here, loyalty and dedication may be more important than passion.

Capricorn rules the knees, joints, ligaments and bones in general, teeth, hair, and the epidermis.

Sun in Aquarius–January 21 to February 18

I know.

Symbol: The Water Bearer
Planetary Ruler: Uranus
Element: Air
Quality: Fixed
Complementary Sign: Leo

Traditionally known as the sign of hope and the sign of humanity, Aquarius, the Water-Bearer, symbolizes universal brotherhood, spiritual nourishment, objective truth, and social justice. Altruism motivates many Aquarians' actions, and they seek alliances with like-minded groups and individuals. Rarely do Aquarians accomplish their aims by their own actions, and their success depends upon their influence and the quality of those with whom they are associated. Their interest in and sympathy for the human condition wins the respect and confidence of those around them. Ruled by Uranus, freedom is very important to Aquarians, and yet those they befriend benefit from the unswerving Aquarian loyalty.

Although a fixed sign, Aquarians can be eccentric as well as determined and stubborn. Bizarre behavior and eccentricity for its own sake are an arrested or retarded application of Aquarian consciousness. Egalitarian in outlook and nature, Aquarians tend to be intolerant of affectation, snobbery, and hypocrisy. They like to act as equals among equals. They derive an honest enjoyment in meeting new people and exchanging ideas. Aquarians relate to others on a mental level. Reason rather than emotion is their strength and means. They are good friends of both sexes, and see no reason for giving up a friendship, say, because of the possessive concerns of marriage.

They represent, idealistically, the angels of the Zodiac, the spiritually and mentally androgynous individual who transcends the barriers of sex, race, creed, and culture. They are the true advocates of both platonic and universal love. It can be said that Aquarius's heart belongs to the world.

Weaker Aquarians often have to learn how to assert themselves in a decisive manner and how to aid others while retaining their own individuality. When objective and ordered, Aquarius acquires the willpower to act with freedom and breadth. Originality enhanced by positive and creative relationships, along with a vision of the future, mark the brilliance of Aquarius at its shining best. Galileo, Charles Darwin, and Abraham Lincoln are among the finest examples of the Aquarian principle at work upon the world.

Aquarians' outward appearance of calm and detachment can be deceptive. Inwardly, they are prone to levels of anxiety that can make them ill. They take their work extremely seriously and are often nervous and apprehensive. They work best in partnerships or with organizations that are attempting to realize some ideal in which their accumulated knowledge, excellent memories, love of freedom, and humanitarianism can find their outward expression.

Romantically, Aquarius seeks a partner who is as much a friend as a lover. Many Aquarians tend to be experimental when it comes to love and are frustrated and disappointed when their partner turns out to be too insular or inadaptable. The Water-Bearer places great value on intellectual rapport in a relationship.

Aquarius rules the lower legs, the calves and ankles, and blood circulation.

Sun in Pisces—February 19 to March 20

I believe.

Symbol: The Two Fishes
Planetary Rulers: Neptune and Jupiter
Element: Water
Quality: Mutable
Complementary Sign: Virgo

Pisces, the twelfth and last sign, is said to unconsciously possess the experience and knowledge of the eleven other signs that have come before it. It is the final stage on the wheel before the beginning of the new cycle, which starts once again with Aries. In that sense, as was stated earlier, Pisces is both the end and the beginning. Pisces is able to understand, transmute, and transcend emotional and psychic problems. In Cancer, the first water sign, emotional and sexual problems are either contained in the subconscious or repressed. In the next water sign, Scorpio, the struggle is to face and release them from the instinctive control of the subconscious as an act of will. In Pisces, the challenge is to comprehend and transcend all the negative passions and emotions that are essentially unconscious in origin and that bind and limit us and cause problems in our relationships with others. Pisces only becomes the sign of suffering and bondage when it fails to do this. In the deep ocean in which Pisces dwells, the individual either sinks or swims. In Pisces we find both the weakest and strongest, often together in a conflicted duality, as symbolized by its sign of two fish swimming in opposite directions, clearly a Western or Middle Eastern depiction of the Chinese Taoist *t'ai chi* symbol, the circle divided into light and dark, yang and yin, the primal beginning of all things.

Nearly all Pisces individuals will experience personal suffering in life. This is part of the Pisces lesson, to be able to feel sympathy for others on a visceral as well as mental level. Pisces attains a broad understanding of the human condition along with the ability to aid and heal the less fortunate and is thus said to be the sign of compassion. The idea is that the Piscean purpose is to mitigate, bring relief, and help others. Some form of personal sacrifice or expression of humility for the benefit of the world seems to be required of nearly every Piscean.

Pisces is sensitive to the emotional nuances of others, and the more highly developed of this sign are able to identify and combat unconscious forces with great powers of penetration and perception.

Weaker Neptunians can be prone to too much secrecy, along with an exaggerated concern with intangible and imaginary forces as a means of escaping from the responsibilities of daily life. Some may turn to an overreliance on the occult, intoxicating substances, dishonest practices, overindulgence in food and sex, and other self-depreciating habits. In this negative mode, Pisces must overcome a morbid sense of fatalism or victimization and realize that they are not chained to a destiny that is not of their own making.

This same impulse to seek oblivion, to escape into a dream world, when positively directed and controlled, can lead to a rich and productive life of the imagination, producing admirable artistic abilities. Many excellent writers, musicians, singers, painters, sculptors, and dancers are born under the sign of Pisces. On an esoteric or archetypal level, Pisces represents the high priest of the temple, the attendant of the Holy Grail who guards its secrets with his life.

Pisces rules the feet, traditionally associated with the understanding of man. In Sophocles' play, *Oedipus the King*, the feet of the newborn child of Laius and Jocasta are riveted together by an iron pin. The child, Oedipus, is then given to a hunter who is ordered to cast him out on a mountainside to die because of a prophecy that Oedipus will kill his father and marry his mother. The hunter does not have the heart to abandon the child and delivers him to the queen of Corinth. Having reached young adulthood, Oedipus, traveling on foot toward Thebes, encounters the Sphinx and successfully answers its riddle (those who fail, die): What creature walks on four legs in the morning, two at midday, then three in the evening? The answer: Man. Intuition combined with reason thus brings about the destruction of the Sphinx, the female riddler. He then meets a belligerent stranger at a place where three roads meet (the sexual area of the body), whom he slays. This stranger, unbeknown to Oedipus, is his father, Laius. Upon reaching Thebes, he falls in love with and marries his mother. The play is a questioning of man's fate versus free will, one of our most ancient and primordial dramas and an issue of great moral concern to the Hellenic Greeks and utterly Piscean in its questions and concerns. The name Oedipus comes from the Greek word meaning "swollen foot," a result of his riveted ankles. Another potent example of Piscean symbolism is that of Mary Magdalene washing the feet of Christ and drying them with her hair.

Pisces are acutely sensitized to the whole of human suffering and possess the ability to see the truth behind symbol and ritual. This sign also stands for the marketplace to which traders, buyers, and pilgrims travel from all over the world.

In marriage, Pisces seeks loving support, a "soul mate" who understands the Piscean need for creative solitude or privacy, while matching the depth of emotion and passion that Pisces brings to its relationships. Trust and loyalty are very important to them, as they tend to be blind to the faults of those they love.

Pisces rules the feet, the lymphatic system, and fatty tissues.

THE SUN IN THE HOUSES

The Sun in the houses represents the areas of life most strongly affected by expressions of individual power and will.

The Sun in the 1st House

The Sun in the 1st House indicates abundant vitality combined with a strong will and intense self-awareness. Initiative, leadership, ambition, and self-determination, the desire to follow one's own course, are highly characteristic. These individuals possess great reserves of energy and strong recuperative powers that enable them to overcome physical afflictions and ailments of almost every kind. Distinction and esteem are of paramount importance to them, and they will work long and hard to achieve it. If the Sun is afflicted in the 1st House, the individual can suffer from excessive pride, egotism, compulsiveness, and the desire to dominate or rule others.

The Sun in the 2nd House

The Sun in the 2nd House indicates how the individual uses money and other material resources. Here, the proper management and utilization of money and property must be learned. The Sun sign position is a strong indicator of how income and resources are acquired and used.

If the Sun is afflicted in the 2nd House, there can be an exaggerated concern with wealth and material gains at the expense of other values. These persons may also frivolously squander their wealth in the name of self-aggrandizement and ego gratification.

The Sun in the 3rd House

Here we see a strong drive to achieve distinction through intellectual brilliance and accomplishments. A strong scientific bent may be indicated. Owing to their curiosity, these individuals have a strong desire to travel and are eager to investigate anything new, especially when it is related to matters ruled by the Sun sign and their particular field of activity. Brothers, sisters, friends, and neighbors mostly likely play major roles in their lives, and the ability to clearly express and communicate their ideas is very important to them. If the Sun is afflicted in the 3rd House, the individual may suffer from arrogance and intellectual snobbery, with a tendency to impose his or her ideas on others.

The Sun in the 4th House

A secure home and family is extremely important to the Sun in the 4th-House individual. They tend to be proud of their family heritage and wish for their homes to be the showpieces by which they are perceived and judged. The first part of their lives may often be a difficult struggle to obtain the property they desire, with increasing prosperity and security coming later in life. The Sun in the 4th House indicates a strong interest in real estate (land and houses), ecology, and natural resources.

When the Sun is afflicted in the 4th House, there may be excessive family pride, conflict with parents, and a desire to dominate and even tyrannize the domestic scene.

The Sun in the 5th House

Here we see a joyful love of life and a strong drive for creative self-expression. These individuals are highly competitive, inclined toward sports and artistic pursuits. They seek pleasure and romance with others, have radiant dispositions, and tend to attract many friends. They wish to be noticed and appreciated. They can, however, sometimes appear as egocentric, overly dramatic, petulant, and childish—haughty prima donnas.

People with a 5th-House Sun are ardent lovers, and falling in love can be all-consuming for them. In spite of their highly amorous natures, they are very capable of being loyal to one person. They have a great love of children, although, if the Sun is in one of the fire signs, they may have few or none of their own.

The Sun in the 6th House

People with the Sun in the 6th House seek fulfillment and distinction through their work and service, in which they take great pride. Their self-esteem is related directly to their work. If their work is not outwardly recognized or appreciated, they can become resentful toward their employers. Employees with the Sun in this position will demand rights and privileges, while employers with the Sun in the 6th House can be exacting and authoritarian.

The Sun in the 6th House tends to indicate delicate health, with the need to pay careful attention to diet and exercise. If the Sun is well aspected, the individual has an intuitive understanding of how to maintain his or her health. There may even be an interest in a health-related career such as nursing or medicine. Good employment is rarely a problem, unless the Sun is afflicted, in which case long periods of unemployment can be the result.

The Sun in the 7th House

The Sun in the 7th House indicates a strong capacity for close personal relationships. When the Sun is well aspected, the individual attracts strong and loyal friends. Marriage is of paramount importance and can add to greater success in life. When the Sun is afflicted, there can be a tendency to dominate or be dominated by one's partner, with a need to learn cooperation and respect for others.

The Sun in the 8th House

The Sun in the 8th House points to an underlying interest in the mysteries of life, especially death, the transmigration of the soul, and other notions pertaining to the continuation of consciousness and the possibility of an afterlife. Spiritual growth and self-improvement come as a result of conscious will. In all likelihood, the individual will have direct personal experience of a deeper reality beyond material circumstances, making him or her fearless in the knowledge of life's fundamental principles. Much can be required and much can be gained. On a more mundane level, there will be concerns with such material matters as taxes, insurance, inheritance, and the finances and assets of one's partner. It can indicate inheritances and legacies or, if afflicted, troubles with these matters, including divorce settlements.

The Sun in the 9th House

The Sun's position in the 9th House shows a dynamic interest in spiritual, religious, and philosophical pursuits. The intuitive intellect is developed, active, and capable of insights that can border on the prophetic. There is a keen interest in international affairs and foreign countries and their cultures, often accompanied by a strong desire to travel. If the Sun is in one of the fixed signs—Taurus, Leo, Scorpio, or Aquarius—the urge to travel may be greatly reduced. If Leo is on the 4th House cusp, the individual will most likely end up living far from his or her childhood home.

The Sun in the 10th House

The Sun here denotes strong ambition to attain positions of power and authority. Many politicians have the Sun in the 10th House. Along with the drive for power comes an enhanced sense of social responsibility. There is a strong desire for honor and recognition, and a capacity to work hard in order to achieve the desired success. Often, these individuals are born into families of high social standing and possess an acute sense of personal dignity and the importance of moral integrity. When the Sun is afflicted, the opposite is true; they can be ruthless and unscrupulous in their drive for power and subject to public disgrace.

The Sun in the 11th House

Here we find an interest and concern with friendships and group relationships and activities. There is a strong interest in scientific endeavors and inventions, as well as in matters related to the occult. When the Sun is well aspected, the individual will have many friends and be held in high esteem. Humanitarian feelings are strong, with a deeply rooted and impartial belief in individual dignity and human rights. If the Sun is afflicted, there can be a tendency to dominate others, often for selfish motives. The individual can also be easily deceived or led astray by others.

The Sun in the 12th House

Here the will is directed toward exploring and understanding one's personal inner life, with a keen interest in psychology and psychic research. These individuals are often quiet and retiring, to the extent that they can be isolated and lonely. However, they can find fulfillment through service to others. If the Sun is afflicted in the 12th House, there can be excessive shyness, neurosis, and a desire to control others through secret or clandestine means. There may also be secret enemies lurking in the shadows.

THE SUN IN ASPECT

Aspects of the Sun all reflect in some way the fundamental self and the nature and use of willpower.

Sun Conjunctions

Sun conjunctions denote willpower, initiative, and creative abilities in regard to the affairs ruled by the planet or planets forming the conjunction and the signs and houses in which the conjunction is found. Whether this is positive or negative depends on the other aspects made to the conjunction and the planets involved.

Sun Sextiles

Sextiles of the Sun represent opportunities for creative self-expression and mental growth and development in regard to the affairs ruled by the Sun in its house and sign position, by the planet or planets forming the sextile, and the houses they occupy and rule.

Sun Squares

Sun squares indicate difficulties and obstacles in the wise and harmonious use of willpower. Difficulties and frustrations will be encountered in the affairs ruled by the planet or planets involved in the square and in the houses and signs the Sun and the planet(s) occupy and rule.

Sun Trines

Trines of the Sun point to good fortune in the affairs ruled by the Sun and the planet or planets forming the trine and the houses they rule and occupy. In general, Sun trines favor love relationships. Benefits come through all things related to the Sun, such as education, the arts, and children.

Sun Oppositions

Oppositions to the Sun indicate conflicts of will between the individual and those ruled by the planet or planets forming the opposition. The nature of these conflicts is determined by the signs and houses which the Sun and the opposing planet(s) rule and occupy.

CHAPTER 6

THE MOON

The Moon relates to the unconscious, all things emotional and feminine, or yin, and often, along with the Ascendant, tells us a great deal about the physical body as it represents what we put into it in the form of nourishment.

THE MOON IN THE SIGNS

The Moon in the signs tells us about how life's situations tend to affect us on the emotional level, about family and early childhood and how those formative experiences color our emotional outlook.

The Moon in Aries

Those with the Moon in Aries are likely to be emotionally volatile and impulsive. They may experience sudden flare-ups of temper that quickly pass and a tendency to act precipitously without any regard for consequences. These individuals are extremely willful and independent. They have a tendency to dominate others emotionally and are prone to take things personally.

The Moon in Taurus

The Moon in Taurus indicates that emotional well-being is based primarily on financial and material security. The Moon in this sign attracts wealth. The individual will have a fondness for good food and comfortable surroundings, but will also show great common sense in handling financial and domestic affairs. His or her emotions are generally steady and placid. When the Moon is afflicted, the person can be rigid and stubborn and may show a tendency toward laziness and an excessive attachment to material comforts.

The Moon in Gemini

Here we will find a temperament that is highly emotional and vacillating, although quick-witted and resourceful, with the ability to come up with solutions to practical problems through rational analysis. The Moon in Gemini can make for an incessant talker. These individuals are highly mental and inclined to rationalize their emotions to the point of not really knowing what they feel. They are extremely restless, likely to travel a great deal, and change their homes often or even have more than one home. When the Moon is afflicted, emotions can distort reason, and they may experience both mental and emotional confusion.

The Moon in Cancer

The Moon in Cancer indicates strong ties to the mother, the family, and the home. Here, marriage and domestic security are important to emotional well-being. These individuals are extremely sensitive to the moods of others, often to the point of being psychic. They make good homemakers, parents, and cooks. When the Moon is afflicted, they can be manipulative and domineering, especially with their children, and even emotionally unstable.

The Moon in Leo

Here there is a strong unconscious need to be appreciated and admired, coupled with an equally strong need for romance and affection. These individuals are especially fond and protective of their children and love entertainment in all its forms. They are extremely proud and can be self-centered, stubborn, and also highly susceptible to flattery. Self-dramatization is a common characteristic with the Moon in Leo, along with a tendency to dominate others. However, their need to love and be loved is the fundamental driving force that mitigates this dramatic energy.

The Moon in Virgo

An exacting and hardworking personality is indicated by the Moon in Virgo. Neatness and hygiene are of particular concern to these individuals, along with diet and health. They tend to be shy and retiring, preferring to work quietly behind the scenes, and happy to serve as dedicated and thorough workers. If the Moon is afflicted, there can be an obsession with cleanliness, order, and inconsequential details along with a quarrelsome and highly critical attitude.

The Moon in Libra

Those born with the Moon in Libra will be distinguished by their personal elegance and good manners. They are courteous and gracious to everyone, as their self-esteem is in large part dependent on the approval of others. Coarseness and vulgarity in any form are upsetting to them, as are any conflicts in their relationships, which can actually have an adverse effect on their health. When the Moon is afflicted here, they can be too easily influenced by and subservient to the opinions and approval of others—especially their marriage partners—and depend too much on others for their emotional security. Often, the Moon in Libra indicates a strong link to the mother. With their charm and grace, these individuals can shine in areas concerned with public relations.

The Moon in Scorpio

The Moon in Scorpio indicates a sensual nature and the strong pursuit of personal pleasures, along with a proclivity for sexual adventures. However, strong and biased emotions based on willful desire and a tendency to take personal affairs extremely seriously—often leading to possessiveness and jealously—can also arise from the Moon in Scorpio. These people don't easily forget or forgive personal affronts, and they may have a tendency to brood and become obsessed with revenge. Given their strong desires, they can be stubborn and unyielding. However, when positively aspected, the Moon in Scorpio sees no sacrifice as too great in achieving a worthwhile objective.

The Moon in Sagittarius

Those with the Moon in Sagittarius are by nature idealistic. They have high aspirations but often lack a realistic sense of how to achieve them. They adhere strongly to the religious and philosophical beliefs instilled in them by their parents. As a result, when afflicted, they can be narrow-minded, dogmatic, and judgmental, lacking in compassion and objectivity. On the bright side, they can be optimistic, cheerful, adventurous, and curious about the world, with a love of travel and meeting new people. Often, they will take up residence in a foreign country or somewhere far from their original home.

The Moon in Capricorn

Capricorn Moon individuals are highly ambitious and hard-working, active seekers of wealth and status both for themselves as well as for their family. Often they are late bloomers, with success finally being achieved as a result of the many lessons learned during the long climb to the top. The Moon shows our emotions, and Capricorn's ruler, Saturn, places a kind of cold efficiency on the Moon's feelings. However, due to Capricorn being a feminine sign, the Moon here can be as emotional as in any other sign. Capricorn is also the sign of ambition and organization. Washington, Lincoln, Bismarck, Thomas Edison, Ayn Rand, and Robert Kennedy all had Capricorn Moons. With the Moon in Capricorn there is an emotional need to be organized and get the job done. These individuals may be insecure about their own worth and overly sensitive to real or imagined criticisms and slights. Their life is based on personal dignity and ambition. With an afflicted Moon, they can be calculating and ruthless in their drive to succeed, with little or no respect for the feelings and desires of others.

The Moon in Aquarius

Here we see a direct concern for and ability to sympathize with the needs of humanity. Freedom of expression, both intellectual and emotional, and freedom within relationships are of utmost importance to persons born with the Moon in Aquarius. They are most likely to have unusual or nonconformist marriages. Their homes are gathering places for friends and group activities. When negative, there can be an irrational need for freedom at any cost, a fear of close personal relationships, and even a tendency to emotional perversity.

The Moon in Pisces

These individuals can be highly sensitive and psychic, able to absorb the thoughts and feelings of others, at times to the point of being mediumistic. They have vivid imaginations and are often poetically, musically, or artistically gifted. Generally, they are kind and sympathetic owing to their sensitivity to others. Their extreme impressionability on the unconscious or intuitive level, however, can make them psychologically vulnerable if they do not know how to protect themselves emotionally. If the Moon is afflicted, they can be highly neurotic and even suffer from psychotic conditions.

THE MOON IN THE HOUSES

The Moon in the houses reflects the unconscious habits of the past and the department of life in which we react unconsciously to environmental stimuli as well as to other people. The Moon's house position can also indicate the types of activities that are likely to occur in our homes.

The Moon in the 1st House

Here, the individual's self-awareness and expression are strongly colored by his or her emotions and childhood conditioning. These persons' moods and responses can be highly changeable, and they can lack a clear sense of direction and purpose. Often, other people have a strong influence on personal identity and can become involved in their personal affairs.

The Moon in the 2nd House

Here, a strong need for financial security and a stable home and family are indicated. Emotional well-being in general is dependent on material comfort. The individual is likely to have good business sense, especially in matters of real estate and property. If the Moon is in a fixed sign or an earth sign, there will be a strong ability to make and hold onto money.

The Moon in the 3rd House

Those with the Moon in the 3rd House have insatiable curiosity and are constantly on the move. They have a tendency to daydream and fantasize, and their thoughts and speech are strongly influenced by emotional factors arising from early childhood and family relationships. In fact, their familial relationships influence their entire outlook and much of their activity is likely to involve brothers and sisters.

The Moon in the 4th House

As the 4th House relates to the sign Cancer, which is ruled by the Moon, this position indicates a strong emotional attachment to home and family. Parents, especially the mother, represent a strong influence. These individuals will almost always be especially fond of cooking and housekeeping, and they can also prosper in businesses related to food, domestic products, and real estate. If the Moon is afflicted, they may experience a lack of domestic harmony and stability. If well situated, financial prospects are more likely to be better in the second half of life.

The Moon in the 5th House

The Moon in this house can indicate fertility and child bearing, especially if it is in a water sign. These individuals are often very fond of children. Their romantic attractions are based on emotional needs, making them emotionally dependent on their partners. Their affections may be changeable or capricious if there is emotional instability.

The Moon in the 6th House

The Moon in the 6th House can mean that the individual's health is strongly influenced by emotional states, making him or her inclined to hypochondria or psychosomatic illness. Emotional states can also have a positive or negative effect on work and business relationships. Those with an afflicted Moon here may change jobs often, and employers with this Moon may find it difficult to retain reliable or permanent employees. Diet is of major importance to health and well-being, and these individuals can be skilled at food preparation.

The Moon in the 7th House

With the Moon in the 7th House, there is a strong likelihood of marrying for emotional and domestic security rather than for purely romantic concerns. These individuals seek emotional fulfillment through their relationships and are therefore heavily influenced by them. Frequently, they seek a mother or father figure in their partner.

The Moon in the 8th House

The Moon in this position often indicates a concern with inheritance, insurance, and property taxes, and these matters may also involve an important woman in the individual's life. Financial affairs are greatly affected through marriage or partnerships. These individuals may also have a highly developed psychic sensitivity and an awareness of invisible forces that may lead to an interest in the occult. The 8th House is ruled by Pluto and related to the sign Scorpio, which rules the sex organs. Scorpio and the 8th House are also ruled by Mars, the planet of desire. If the Moon is afflicted here, emotional desires can lead to an overemphasis on sex and sensuality.

The Moon in the 9th House

Those with the Moon in the 9th House will place great value on the social, religious, and ethical values instilled in them from early childhood. If the Moon is afflicted, a narrow and dogmatic social and religious bias can be the result, with the individual's convictions based more on emotion than reason. When positive, this is the house of the higher mind, of reason and understanding. These people will travel often and are inclined to take up residence far from their place of birth.

The Moon in the 10th House

The need to achieve prominence and recognition is the driving factor for those born with the Moon in this position. Often they come from families of high social standing and inherited ambition. The influence of the mother is especially dominant, and their careers tend to be assisted or enhanced by women. If positively aspected, it is a particularly good position for those with political ambitions.

The Moon in the 11th House

The Moon in this house provides a strong desire for friendship and group acceptance and activities. Many friendships are made through family associations, and there will also be many friendships of a purely platonic nature with members of the opposite sex. Emotional states are influenced by the opinions and reactions of others, and companionship is essential for emotional well-being.

The Moon in the 12th House

With the Moon in the 12th House, moods and emotions are strongly affected by the unconscious and the memories of past experiences. These individuals can be highly psychic and intuitive. If the Moon is afflicted here, they may experience extreme emotional sensitivity, neurotic tendencies, shyness, and loneliness. If the Moon rules the 5th, 7th, or 8th Houses (i.e., if Cancer is found on these house cusps), or strongly aspects Venus or the ruler of the 5th House, these individuals may find themselves involved in clandestine love affairs.

ASPECTS OF THE MOON

The Moon represents the passive feminine principle, that aspect of consciousness which is receptive to outside influences. It is a strong indicator of how we react to other people. Aspects of the Moon are all reflections of the unconscious mind, behavior patterns formed by the past, and automatic reactions. The Moon is connected to memory, especially regarding emotional experiences, and the Moon's aspects are a strong indicator of our ability to store information. In a man's horoscope, lunar aspects indicate the way he reacts to women. In a woman's horoscope, the Moon represents the way basic feminine and maternal qualities are expressed, including female physical and emotional health (the Moon being related to the female menstrual cycle). In both male and female horoscopes, the Moon represents the influence of the mother.

Moon Conjunctions

Moon conjunctions point to intense feelings and emotions regarding the affairs ruled by the planet or planets involved and the signs and houses they occupy and rule. Domestic life, parents, and even food will be strongly influenced by the affairs governed by these planets. In these areas, the individual will be prone to acting out of unconscious impulse and early childhood conditioning. Women will exert a strong influence on the individual in the affairs ruled by the conjunction.

Moon Sextiles

Moon sextiles indicate an opportunity for growth and development in the affairs ruled by the planet or planets forming the sextile and the signs and houses the Moon and the planet(s) occupy and rule. Often, women play a significant role in furthering the individual's progress. Moon sextiles mean good emotional communication and friendship with women in general and especially the mother.

Moon Squares

Squares of the Moon point to emotional blockages and frustrations that are the product of early childhood and heredity. Often there is an unconscious resentment of women resulting from conflicts with the mother, along with racial and social prejudices, all of which greatly hinder the individual's capacity for emotional freedom and happiness.

Moon Trines

Trines of the Moon indicate unconscious conditioning and behavioral patterns that work to the benefit of the individual's social progress, especially regarding women. These benefits come through the affairs ruled by the planet or planets that form the trine and the houses and signs occupied and ruled by the Moon and the planet(s) involved. These trines generally indicate a happy childhood and harmonious family life.

Moon Oppositions

Oppositions of the Moon indicate emotional problems in relationships. The individual may tend to project his or her own emotional problems and faults onto others. Objectivity and emotional detachment must be exercised regarding the affairs ruled by the planet or planets forming the opposition and the signs and houses occupied and ruled by the planet(s).

CHAPTER 7

MERCURY

Mercury is the ruler of our thought processes and communication. As mentioned earlier, it is never more than 28 degrees from the Sun. It expresses itself most effectively, however, when it is at least 3 degrees from the Sun.

MERCURY IN THE SIGNS

Mercury's sign position reveals the psychological patterns and perceptions behind our ability to make judgments and decisions and convey ideas to others, as well as what tends to occupy our thoughts.

Mercury in Aries

These individuals are able to think originally, quickly, and decisively and are inclined to show a fondness for competitive argument and debate. They can, however, be intellectually egotistical and stubborn, impulsive in their judgments and decisions, and highly personal in their point of view. They are impatient with opposition and delay and can become quick-tempered or irritable.

Mercury in Taurus

These individuals possess much in the way of simple common sense, their thought processes concentrated on that which is of practical and material concern. They have great powers of concentration, enabling them to shut out or ignore anything that may distract them from the object of their focus. They have an almost uncanny ability to simply not perceive whatever they don't want to be bothered with, which can make them blind to matters they should recognize for their own good. Thus they can be shortsighted and stubborn. If Mercury is well aspected, these individuals can have considerable mental abilities in the arts, mathematics, and physical science, owing to the Taurian-Venusian sense of structure and form interpreted through Mercury's mental understanding. If Mercury is afflicted here, the individual may have to struggle with materialism, avarice, and intellectual obstinacy.

Mercury in Gemini

Here, Mercury is in the sign of its rulership. When well aspected, pure and logical reason reaches its highest expression. Mercury in Gemini is lucid, versatile, mentally agile and perceptive, concerned with objective facts and unbiased truth. These individuals will be knowledgeable in a wide variety of subjects and will be distinguished by their ability to communicate eloquently and precisely in both speech and writing. They have immense curiosity and are highly sensitive to outside stimuli, registering everything around them with vivid intensity. Their nerves can become frayed or overloaded by the abundance of information they are receiving, which can further result in confusion, fatigue, and irritability.

If Mercury is afflicted, these individuals can be prone to incessant trivial chatter and an inability to focus.

Mercury in Cancer

Mercury in Cancer can indicate a mind that is easily influenced by deep-rooted emotions and unconscious desires, sometimes resulting in bias, prejudice, and a lack of objectivity. If Mercury is afflicted here, the individual can be prone to dishonesty without even realizing it. On the other hand, an unafflicted Mercury in Cancer can result in a very good memory owing to the emotional intensity associated with its thoughts and an ability to absorb information subliminally, almost as though through osmosis. Much of the mental processes here actually occur more on the unconscious level, as Cancer brings the lunar element to Mercury. These individuals can be highly sensitive and very susceptible to the opinions and attitudes of those around them. Much of their thinking is centered on home and family.

Mercury in Leo

A strong will and fixed purpose are indicated here, along with self-confidence and the ability to focus and concentrate. There can, however, be a tendency to overlook anything that does not relate immediately to the matter at hand and to deal with things in general terms while ignoring important details. Those with Mercury in Leo have a strong desire to be regarded as experts or authorities in their chosen fields, and they can be dramatic and forceful in their self-expression. Naturally, if taken to the extreme, this can result in excessive pride and arrogance. Leo being a fixed sign, opinions are formed slowly and, once formed, are difficult to change.

These individuals are generally extremely positive when it comes to tackling and solving problems and often possess considerable executive abilities. They can make gifted teachers, especially when working with children.

Mercury in Virgo

Here we will find great analytical powers and practical reasoning, with a concern for precision and detail that can appear as neurotic or trivial to others. Order and efficiency, especially in work, is of major concern for Mercury in Virgo. Professional and financial success is achieved by acquiring a good education and specialist skills. Interest in and knowledge of language and grammar can make these people eloquent and precise in speech and writing. They will be especially concerned with correct word use, spelling, grammar, and punctuation. Mercury in Virgo is not concerned with ideas for their own sake (like Mercury in Gemini), but with their practical application. These individuals are work-oriented and can tend to be shy and retiring, with little interest in idle conversation. When badly aspected, Mercury in Virgo's concern for details can assume undue importance and blind these individuals to the overall matter at hand. Medicine, mathematics, diet, hygiene, and any other work requiring precision and detail will be of interest.

Mercury in Libra

Here, the primary mental concern is with human relationships and psychology based on an innate and keen interest in the thought and behavior patterns of others. These individuals tend to naturally excel in such fields as sociology, psychology, public relations, law, and even astrology. Good communication and harmonious relationships are essential to them, and they work best when in partnership with others. They are easy to communicate with and have a genuine concern for and interest in the opinions of other people. They are imbued with a strong sense of justice and honesty and will consider all sides of an issue before making a decision. When Mercury here is afflicted, this careful weighing and consideration can lead to indecisiveness. When these people do make decisions, however, they are generally thoughtful and just.

Honesty, good manners, and refinement of thought and gesture are of utmost importance to them. They find rough or uncouth speech and behavior and dishonesty and unfairness extremely distasteful and will avoid them whenever possible. They are highly sensitive to the odors, personal appearance, and mannerisms of others. Inappropriate dress and coarse language can be regarded by them as personal and social affronts. Although gentle and considerate in their dealings with others, Mercury in Libra people can be strict and unyielding when it comes to their own principles. When negative or superficial, however, they can appear to lack conviction as a result of their tendency to simply agree with others in order to gain approval or avoid conflict.

Mercury in Scorpio

This is a highly intuitive mind capable of profound insight and critical analysis of human motivations. Secretive and resourceful, with an acute understanding of "what lies beneath," these individuals make good detectives, investigators, and researchers. They are capable of surmounting obstacles and solving problems that others find impossible to even broach. They possess an innate curiosity about the inner workings of things and the hidden mysteries of life. When negative, they can be furtive, scheming, mistrustful of others, and preoccupied with sex.

Mercury in Sagittarius

These individuals will be forthright in their speech and demand absolute intellectual freedom, although their ideas rarely depart from traditional concepts or accepted codes of social behavior. Here the major mental concern is with social or collective codes of thought, whether religious, legal, or philosophical. As they are concerned with ideas rather than facts, these people are often insightful in their understanding of social forces and the subsequent unfolding of events. This can at times make them seem almost prophetic. They have a strong desire to be seen as paragons of truth and to be respected within their communities, an urge that can lead to moral hypocrisy and pedantry if Mercury is afflicted and conformity carried too far.

Mercury in Capricorn

Here is a mind that is ambitious, shrewd, practical, organized, and determined to achieve success in the material world.

These individuals are methodical in thought and action, their reasoning thorough and cautious, although not particularly original. They are patient and disciplined, often gifted in math, and have good management abilities. They tend to be politically conservative and defenders of the established social order, as they have a deep-rooted respect for that which has stood the test of time. Like Virgo, another earth sign, Mercury in Capricorn holds ideas as important only in regard to their practical application. They are realistic rather than idealistic. If Mercury is afflicted in this sign, there is a danger of avarice and an inclination to use people unscrupulously to attain material goals. Seriousness and discipline can also result in sternness and a very unappealing lack of humor.

Mercury in Aquarius

Here the mind is totally open to new experiences. The world is viewed from the point of view of objective and impersonal truth. There is little tolerance or regard for tradition or social mores if they conflict with or deny the objective facts and the evidence of firsthand experience. Owing to their objectivity, very little surprises these people, and they readily accept and acknowledge what others may find incomprehensible or even world shattering. They are capable of receiving ideas from the archetypal realm of the collective and universal consciousness and are often telepathic. They also tend to make excellent scientists. Their ability to perceive things in broad terms gives them a decidedly humanitarian outlook. They like to work in conjunction with others and seek mental stimulation through friendship.

Mercury in Pisces

Mercury in Pisces endows a vivid imagination along with a photographic ability to visualize thoughts and memories. These individuals tend to be highly intuitive and telepathic. They are, as a result, easily influenced by subliminal suggestion as they unconsciously tune in to the thoughts and feelings of those around them. Conclusions are reached not through rational thought but through impressions and perceptions that rise up from the layers of the unconscious. Like Mercury in Cancer, the mind can become biased by unconscious emotional patterns based on past experiences. If Mercury is afflicted, there is the danger of the mind being trapped in memory to the point that perception is distorted, resulting in neurosis. On the other hand, this extreme sensitivity and insight can result in great literary, artistic, and visionary abilities.

These people are capable of great sympathy for and empathy with others. Pisces is a mutable sign, and this can cause emotional fluctuations, vacillation when it comes to decision making, and a tendency to daydream. Excessive secrecy and a need for privacy can lead to shyness. If Mercury is afflicted, the imagination can become morbid, and excessive sensitivity can bring on a persecution complex, imagining slights and personal criticisms where none exist.

MERCURY IN THE HOUSES

Mercury in the houses tells us about the practical affairs of daily life that involve our thinking and communication. It also shows what areas of activity will be influenced or affected by these thoughts and communications.

Mercury in the 1st House

Mercury in the 1st House indicates a mind that is curious and inquiring. Very little escapes these individuals' attention. Willpower and mental initiative are hallmarks of Mercury in this position, making these people intellectually competitive. The 1st House indicates self-expression through action. Those with Mercury in the 1st House make good writers, journalists, scientists, researchers, and scholars because of their intelligence and innate ability for self-expression. They are talkative and inclined to write a lot owing to their intense desire to express themselves verbally.

Mercury in the 2nd House

Here, the individual's primary preoccupations will be with business, money, and that which produces practical and concrete results. Education is pursued in the name of earning power, and these individuals can be original and inventive in formulating ways of making money. Economists, entrepreneurs, business advisors, and corporate planners often have Mercury in the 2nd House. Keen business acumen can also be manifested in media-related businesses such as broadcasting, publishing, and telecommunications.

Mercury in the 3rd House

The 3rd House corresponds to Gemini, which Mercury rules, so this strong position endows the individual with a superior intellect and abilities in communication in any variety of forms, with much mental agility and originality. If Mercury is afflicted here by challenging aspects, troubles can arise from indiscreet talk or false or erroneous information; the individual may also experience problems with contracts and agreements. Many short trips and much communication with siblings, relatives, and neighbors are also characteristic of Mercury in the 3rd House.

Mercury in the 4th House

With Mercury in the 4th House, the home is more than likely to be the center of educational and intellectual activity, as well as the place of work. The home will probably have a large library, and the individual may spend much time with his or her family in educational pursuits. Those with Mercury in the 4th House will be concerned with investigating their genealogy and often have well-educated parents. They will probably be interested in real estate, agriculture, and the earth sciences. Also, people who live in trailers or have a nomadic lifestyle are likely to have Mercury in the 4th House. If Mercury is afflicted, intellectual disputes and disagreements with family members may occur.

Mercury in the 5th House

This is the position of writers in general and indicates a keen interest in intellectual and creative endeavors. Here the individual is strongly attracted to all forms of art that convey information. These individuals express themselves forcefully and dramatically and desire to be admired for their artistic or intellectual achievements. They take great pride in their children and are very concerned with their education. Often they are romantically attracted to those they find intellectually exciting and stimulating. If Mercury is afflicted, there can be a tendency toward intellectual conceit, unwise speculations, and a critical and analytical approach to romance, with no partner being mentally up to par.

Mercury in the 6th House

The 6th House corresponds to Virgo, which Mercury rules. Mercury in this position indicates a concern with duty, work, and personal hygiene and appearance. There is a tendency here toward overwork and perfectionism. Methodical and efficient, these individuals keep themselves up with the latest developments in their fields of endeavor and are more than likely specialists in their work. It is an ideal position for those involved in medicine, science, or engineering. They are particularly sensitive to any disorder or chaos in their environment. If Mercury is afflicted, these individuals can be highly critical, obsessively preoccupied with insignificant details, or overly concerned about ill health.

Mercury in the 7th House

The major concern here is with communication and intellectual cooperation with others, with a strong preference for working within a partnership. These individuals are skilled at public communication and are often successful in law, public relations, and sales, as well as having a strong aptitude for psychology, arbitration, mediation, and counseling. They are very concerned with what others think and will seek intellectual companionship with both their friends and romantic partners. Mercury in the 7th House can indicate marriage with an employee, coworker, or even a relative. If Mercury is afflicted, there can be problems in communicating with others, misunderstandings in marriage and partnerships, and broken agreements; all contracts must be carefully considered. With an afflicted 7th-House Mercury, the individual's partner may be unstable or deceptive.

Mercury in the 8th House

Here we find a keen interest in both science and the occult. The 8th House is the house of death, and these interests may well extend into spiritualism and communication with the dead. The best mediums probably have Mercury in the 8th House. Those with Mercury in this position tend to be highly secretive, especially about personal information. They thrive on mystery and intrigue and are particularly gifted in uncovering secrets and exposing the hidden motivations of others. Often it seems that this information simply comes to them by chance or luck. They do not easily forget the slights and wrongful actions of others. If Mercury is afflicted, these people can hold grudges and engage in secret plots for revenge.

Mercury in the 9th House

Mercury in the 9th House means there will be a strong interest in philosophy, law, and higher education, all aimed at acquiring an understanding of the fundamental precepts that govern the prevailing social codes and mores. Decisions are based on ethical and moral considerations as well as practical ones. As with Mercury in Sagittarius, this position indicates a strong concern with prevailing attitudes as well as facts. These people will also love travel and display a curiosity about foreign countries and cultures. If Mercury is afflicted here, the individual may be given to intellectual snobbery and dogmatic and sectarian attitudes and beliefs. When favorably aspected here, Mercury can give prophetic insight into the nature of things to come.

Mercury in the 10th House

Here, education will be pursued in the name of attaining a prestigious and lucrative career. These ambitious individuals are highly organized and able to plan for the future. They are politically astute, able to communicate effectively with the public, and have considerable executive ability. It is the position of distinguished and brilliant politicians. It is also a good position for those engaged in communications media, publishing, writing, and teaching. If Mercury is afflicted, ambition can take precedence over principles.

Mercury in the 11th House

This position of Mercury indicates a love of truth, impartiality, and the ability to judge objectively. These people are often quite original and innovative in their thinking and involved in scientific investigation and humanitarian causes. Their friends will have similar concerns. They are impersonal but friendly, willing to exchange ideas with anyone regardless of their background. Open to all of humanity, they are compassionate and insightful and possess an innate understanding of the broader social issues. If Mercury is afflicted, their ideas can be eccentric and impractical, and the ability to communicate and function with groups can be hampered.

Mercury in the 12th House

Here, thinking is strongly influenced by unconscious memories and habits rooted in past experiences. Conclusions and decisions are often based on feelings and impressions arising through the layers of the subconscious rather than on logic. This can have both positive and negative results. Individuals with Mercury in the 12th House are likely to be highly secretive about their thoughts and feelings and prone to shyness. However, their imaginations are highly active, vivid, and valuable, with original ideas and knowledge often gleaned through intuitive and psychic channels. If Mercury is afflicted, the result can be neurosis, mental illness, and a fixation on the past. An afflicted 12th-House Mercury can also indicate mental blocks and learning difficulties, particularly during childhood.

ASPECTS OF MERCURY

Along with the sign it is in, house position, and the houses it rules (those in which Virgo and Gemini are found), aspects of Mercury indicate the way we think and the kind of mind we possess. Mercury is neutral in terms of mental communication, perception, memory, and reasoning. It is colored by the planets that most closely aspect it, along with the sign and house it is in.

Mercury Conjunctions

Conjunctions of Mercury indicate strong mental abilities in reasoning and communication in the areas ruled by the planet or planets forming the conjunction, the house and sign the conjunction occupies, and the houses and signs ruled by Mercury and the conjuncting planet(s).

Mercury Sextiles

Mercury sextiles indicate opportunities for mental growth and development, along with strong reasoning abilities, in those areas influenced by the planet(s) forming the sextile and the signs and houses that Mercury and the planet(s) occupy and rule. The individual will be especially adept at writing, communicating, forming new friendships, and expressing him- or herself through group associations.

Squares

Squares of Mercury indicate difficulties and mental blockages in learning and communicating in those areas ruled by the planet or planets that form the square and the signs and houses they occupy and rule. Although these individuals may be intelligent, they are prone to being opinionated, stubborn, one-sided, and intellectually arrogant in their point of view.

Mercury Trines

Mercury trines indicate a mind that is inspired, agile, and creative, with great powers of comprehension and the ability to communicate quickly and clearly. Success is achieved in the areas ruled by the planet or planets forming the trine and the signs and houses the planets occupy and rule.

Mercury Oppositions

Mercury oppositions point to difficulties in relationships as a result of conflicting opinions and attitudes and an inability to communicate, especially in those areas ruled by the planet or planets opposing Mercury and the signs and houses occupied and ruled by Mercury and the planet(s).

CHAPTER 8

VENUS

 enus, the planet of love and beauty, provides insight into what we value in people and our attitudes about money, personal possessions, society, and aesthetics.

VENUS IN THE SIGNS

Venus's position in the signs shows how we express our love in intimate relationships, as well as our nature in other social partnerships, and the manner in which we choose to live.

Venus in Aries

Those with Venus in Aries are aggressive in their emotional self-expression and confidently pursue the objects of their desire. They can be competitive in seeking the attention and affections of others. Mars, the ruler of Aries, makes them passionate in love and romance and gives energy to the tender affections of Venus. However, Venus in Aries can also make their affections impulsive and unstable, and these people can be self-centered and demanding. When Venus is afflicted, they can be coarse, ill-mannered, and temperamental when the attention they demand is not forthcoming.

Venus in Taurus

Constant and lasting affections are characteristic of Venus in Taurus. Loyalty and steadfastness, though, may be coupled with possessiveness and jealousy if emotional security is in any way threatened. These individuals are sensual and tactile. They enjoy physical contact with their loved ones as well as comfort, luxury, good food, and opulent surroundings; because of the latter, money is important to them. They place a high value on personal beauty and take great efforts to look as attractive as possible. They have an innate sense of the value of material things and a keen eye for objects of beauty and value. They make great antique dealers and art collectors. Also, with their tactile sense, many sculptors and painters have Venus in this sign. These individuals have a kinship with the earth and a love of nature, especially of plants and trees. Taurus rules the throat and the larynx, and coupled with the beauty and grace of Venus, it often bestows these individuals with resonant, melodious voices.

Venus in Gemini

Venus in Gemini confers a strong desire for varied experience and an innate curiosity about people. As a result, these people will naturally seek variety both in their love and social lives. They are not naturally predisposed to settling down in a steady or permanent relationship, although they are capable of sustained devotion, which may seem like a contradiction, but contradiction is a Gemini characteristic. Given their wit and conversational abilities, they are attracted to agile minds and strong intellects. As with the other air signs, they have pleasant and charming manners and a strong dislike of coarse or crude behavior. If Venus is afflicted, these people may seem inconsistent and fickle in romance, and their values concerning love and marriage can be capricious and superficial.

Venus in Cancer

Here there is deep sensitivity where romantic feelings are concerned, along with a strong desire for both emotional and financial security. Venus in Cancer seeks marriage as a basis for a stable domestic life, placing great value on home and family. The extreme sensitivity of these people can make them easily hurt, and their moods can be fluctuating and unpredictable. They require open demonstrations of affection in order to feel loved and secure. Their homes are places of comfort and beauty and the preferred center of their social activity. Both men and women with Venus in this sign will have strong maternal natures. Women with Venus in Cancer have a delicate femininity and are often highly domestic, cooking and keeping house for those they love. If Venus is afflicted, these individuals may exhibit a maudlin sentimentality and unstable emotional reactions.

Venus in Leo

Those with Venus in Leo are ardent and constant in love. Born romantics, they love courtships that are dramatic and exciting, as they are themselves lovers of life and theatrical in their behavior and personal expression. Their ability to dramatize emotions makes them good actors and actresses. They are warmhearted, outgoing, and affectionate and will have a particular fondness for children. They are deeply loyal to those they choose as worthy of their royal affections and tend to be proud of their partners, with a desire to show them off. They can become jealous and possessive, however, when their partner fails or neglects to pay them the appropriate homage in return. Women in particular with Venus in this position wish to be admired and appreciated and will compete for attention in social situations. They can, indeed, be demanding prima donnas and easily seduced by flattery and attention. If Venus is afflicted, the individual can be selfish, narcissistic, vain, excessively proud, snobbish, and overly concerned with sex. With an afflicted Venus in Leo, the individual's romantic relationships can be shallow, based more on flattering the self than on any deep or profound emotional connection.

Venus in Virgo

Venus in Virgo will tend to analyze emotions and be highly critical of loved ones. This emphasis on critical analysis can inhibit the flow of spontaneous affection as well as hinder the intuitive and natural response to beauty. Those with Venus in Virgo often seek partners with whom they can share their work and intellectual pursuits. However, Venus in this sign is more likely to indicate those who remain single and unmarried owing to their highly critical and exacting standards for a mate. In such cases, their affections may be redirected toward pets or even inanimate objects. These individuals are fastidious when it comes to matters of order, manners, and hygiene. Their extreme sense of social propriety is often a shield hiding feelings of social and sexual inferiority and can prevent them from developing successful romantic relationships, resulting in feelings of frustration, loneliness, and social isolation. If Venus is well placed and well aspected, these tendencies can be overcome or compensated. Venus in Virgo can impart a love of material comforts and possessions of quality and beauty, which these individuals believe impart status. They are capable of being highly sympathetic, with a nurturing instinct and ability that makes them skilled at tending to the sick. Reason and analysis combined with the emotions (Venus in a Mercury-ruled sign) can also bestow gifts in the field of psychotherapy. If Venus is afflicted by Mars, Neptune, Uranus, or Pluto, these individuals may well react against shyness, their feelings of sexual inferiority, and the strictures of social propriety by adopting a loose and promiscuous lifestyle in their search for love and sexual fulfillment, while affirming their own desirability.

Venus in Libra

Marriage and harmonious social relationships are of paramount importance to Venus in Libra. Venus rules Libra and is very powerful here, usually bestowing physical beauty and a natural animal grace that is very attractive to the opposite sex. They have an innate ability to understand the feelings of others, along with a strong desire for companionship and relationships based on a close and harmonious bond. These people have a strong desire to please and a deep consideration for others, along with a sense of justice and fairness in all of their relationships. They have the typical Libran dislike of crudeness and coarse manners, and are themselves gracious and polite. Although romantic and affectionate, like all air signs, they seek mental stimulation in a partner. Disagreements and discord are particularly distasteful to them and they can become nervous, distressed, and even ill if overly exposed to them. Unlike Venus in Taurus, the Libra Venusians seek status through relationships rather than through money and possessions. They have a highly developed sense of aesthetics and are often artistically gifted, especially musically. As an air sign, they generally have keen and precise hearing along with an acute sense of smell. People with Venus afflicted in Libra can appear to lack integrity owing to their desire to avoid conflict at all costs; their social and emotional values can be superficial and conformist. Women with Libra in Venus have a deep desire to be cared for. In public, social propriety is very important to them, and they prefer a restrained and sophisticated approach on the part of the male.

Venus in Scorpio

With Venus in Scorpio, emotions and sexual desires are strong and passionate, often jealous and secretive. These individuals take much pride in sex and romance. In more highly evolved types, idealism, respect, and consideration for the needs of others in close personal relationships and romantic and sexual involvements are prominent. If Venus is afflicted here, it may indicate a dark obsession with sex and sensuality; in close personal relationships, their reactions can be highly emotional, and intense feelings and desires can blind them to others' points of view. If Venus in Scorpio is afflicted in a woman's horoscope, she can be the classic femme fatale who uses her sexual power to manipulate and use others. Venus in this sign can lead to emotional extremes and excesses. On the dark side, they may take romance too seriously. If slighted or rejected, intense jealousy, resentment, and bitterness can be the result. If their love is abused or betrayed, they may respond with hatred or cold indifference. There may also be a strong and dangerous desire to dominate or subtly control a close personal relationship, marriage, or business partner. The intense emotions and desires of Venus in this sign can make for a strong and vivid personality, with an aura of mystery and intrigue. These individuals will be attracted to the occult sciences and life's hidden mysteries and are psychically sensitive to the thoughts and feelings of others.

Venus in Sagittarius

One of the great psychological astrologers, Dane Rudhyar, has noted that each sign is in reaction to and has evolved from the extremes of the sign preceding it. This is particularly true of Venus in Sagittarius. The dark jealousies and intrigues of Venus in Scorpio seem puerile and unevolved to Venus in Sagittarius, which seeks to base its relationships on more objective and ethical principles. These people are vivacious and sociable, outspoken, and frank. Their conduct is ruled by traditional moral structures in which they seek to be open and honest in their relationships. They will often try to convert their spouses or partners to their own religious or moral beliefs simply to have mutually agreed upon rules of conduct. Jupiter's rulership of Sagittarius can make them lavish and flamboyant in their artistic tastes, with a decided attraction to classical forms in both art and music, especially those with a religious or philosophical theme. They gain emotional satisfaction through sports, outdoor activities, and travel. Often, people with Venus in Sagittarius marry foreigners or those of a different race. If Venus is afflicted here, they can be offensively blunt, impractical in their idealism concerning romance, and likely to impose dogmatic beliefs and standards on their loved ones.

Venus in Capricorn

Saturn's rulership of Capricorn may cause those with Venus in this sign to repress their emotions and sexuality, at least in public, for in private they can be highly sensual. Here, wealth and material status are necessary for emotional security. Often, these individuals will seek to improve their status by marrying someone of wealth or social standing. Reserved and dignified, they dislike overt, public displays of emotion and affection. Although not openly demonstrative in their affections, they are loyal and steadfast to their loved ones. If they marry young, they will seek older, more mature partners. If they marry later in life, they will seek younger mates whom they can provide for in return for affection. Like Venus in Sagittarius, they are drawn to classical and traditional art forms. Those with an afflicted Venus in Capricorn may tend toward excessive materialism, emotional coldness, calculating and ulterior motives in relationships, and marriage for money and status with little concern for love.

Venus in Aquarius

Venus in Aquarius is in reaction to the materialism and status-seeking of Venus in Capricorn. Here, the romantic partner must be a friend as well as a lover and understand the Aquarian need for freedom, variety, and mental stimulation. Venus in Aquarius dislikes jealousy and possessiveness and will reject any romantic partner who seeks to restrict his or her social freedom. Romantic attractions can be sudden and casual as opposed to stable and lasting. Intellectual stimulation is important in a romantic partner, and these people are often attracted to ingenious or eccentric types, as well as to those who can expand their social outlets and broaden their horizons. Their attitudes regarding social and sexual morality can be unusual, departing from accepted norms. As with Venus in Gemini and Libra, they have an acute distaste for crude behavior and coarse manners, although they themselves may not necessarily adhere to traditional mores. Their eclecticism can give them unusual aesthetics that are both extremely modern and extremely ancient, a product of Uranus's and Saturn's corulership of Aquarius. They have a highly developed intuition about people's social and emotional dispositions that can at times verge on being telepathic. If Venus is afflicted here, these people can be sexually eccentric and promiscuous, and their emotions can be subject to radical changes, breaking off an old relationship and creating a new one simply out of the desire for greater freedom and new experience. They may be unable to cope with the confines of marriage. Their emotional attitudes can be fixed and stubborn, refusing to see or consider other points of view. If Venus is well aspected, they are capable of sustained and dedicated loyalty to someone they truly love and admire.

Venus in Pisces

With Venus in Pisces, the love principle reaches its highest manifestation on the evolutionary scale of the Zodiac. The universality of Venus in Aquarius combines with the emotional depth and empathy of Pisces to produce an emotional rapport with all life. The experience and knowledge of having passed through all the signs of the Zodiac enable the soul to identify and sympathize with all of humanity. Those with Venus in Pisces are sensitive and romantic. They marry for love and love only. They require clear and demonstrative expressions of love and affection in order not to feel lonely and unappreciated. If such demonstrations are not forthcoming, they may experience feelings of martyrdom which may express themselves religiously or lead to neurosis or mental illness, or all three. Neptune's rulership of Pisces provides intuitive inspiration to Venus, making these people capable of great creative expression in art, poetry, and music that can seem divinely bestowed. Venus in Pisces possibly has more innate ability for inspired artistic expression than any other placement. Owing to their acute emotional sensitivity, these people are often afraid of being hurt by rejection and are therefore reluctant to express their feelings. This can mean that romantic opportunities are sometimes lost. They are inclined to become emotionally dependent on others or have others emotionally dependent on them. If Venus is afflicted, they may lack discrimination in love and be excessively sentimental or hypersensitive, overly dependent on others, lazy, or incapable of objectivity due to blinding emotions.

VENUS IN THE HOUSES

Venus in the houses shows how we express ourselves romantically, socially, and artistically. The house in which Venus is located denotes the type of people with whom we form friendships and social and romantic relationships.

Venus in the 1st House

Those with Venus in the 1st House have personal grace, pleasant manners, and friendly dispositions. It is a position especially beneficial to women, for it bestows physical beauty. It usually indicates a happy childhood and therefore a happy outlook on life. These people are outgoing and aggressive in their efforts to make friends and find lovers. They are fond of anything that enhances their personal appearance, from fine clothes to expensive hair cuts. Their ability to mix well socially provides them with both business and romantic opportunities.

Venus in the 2nd House

Venus in the 2nd House indicates a love of wealth and all the things that money can buy, including social status. These people seek romantic and marriage partners who are wealthy and able to provide the material comforts and luxuries they desire. They are talented in matters of business, especially in business that involves the arts. Women with this position tend to be extravagant, and the men are prone to spend large amounts of money entertaining the women they are courting or even married to. Help comes from friends and social contacts that lead to positions and agreements in business that bring wealth.

Venus in the 3rd House

Venus here indicates a strong interest in artistic and cultural pursuits, with a special love of literature and poetry. Communication skills, especially in speech and writing, are very well developed. A considerable amount of short-distance travel for both business and pleasure is indicated. These individuals have a tendency to intellectually analyze both their romantic and social relationships. They communicate well with their romantic partners and friends and have good relationships with their siblings and neighbors. Often, their social and romantic contacts are made through neighborhood activities and cultural and intellectual pursuits.

Venus in the 4th House

This position denotes a strong attachment to the home, where these individuals prefer to entertain romantic partners and friends in a warm and intimate domestic environment. The home will always be as beautifully decorated as personal means allow. They tend to be close to their parents, through whom much happiness, as well as inheritance, can come. Fourth-House Venus people will have a patriotic love of the natural beauties of their homeland, along with a general love of land, gardening, and beautiful plants and shrubs. Venus in the 4th House holds the promise of being surrounded by beauty and comfort in old age.

Venus in the 5th House

Venus in the 5th House indicates a romantic nature and a love of pleasure and life in general. If Venus is well aspected, the individual will obtain happiness through romance and many romantic opportunities. These people tend to be popular and lovers of, and talented in, the performing arts. Venus in this position bestows a deep love of children and produces loving parents and teachers. Their children are likely to be girls who are artistically talented and physically beautiful.

Venus in the 6th House

With Venus in the 6th House, both friendships and romance are more than likely to come about through work. Working conditions and relationships tend to be pleasant and harmonious. People with Venus in the 6th have a love of beautiful clothing and often ability in dressmaking and fashion design. Although they aren't necessarily robust, their health tends to be good, and it often improves with marriage.

Venus in the 7th House

Here, marriage and close friendships are very important. Marriage is sought in the name of romantic fulfillment, and if Venus is well aspected, the marriage will be happy and harmonious. The 7th-House Venus openly expresses love and consequently receives it in return. These people tend to be very popular because of their pleasant demeanor and consideration for others. They usually marry young and gain financial success through marriage.

Venus in the 8th House

Here we find financial gain through marriage and partnerships. This position tends to indicate an inheritance, unless Venus is afflicted, in which case marriage can be motivated more by financial gain than love, or there can be an overemphasis on sex and sensuality. The intense emotions of the 8th-House Venus can result in jealousy and possessiveness.

Venus in the 9th House

With Venus in the 9th House, the individual has a basic love of philosophy, art, religion, and travel. Marriage partners and friends are met through universities and religious groups, as well as through travel to foreign shores. These people have strong ideals regarding love and may attempt to convert their loved ones to their own beliefs. Generally, they are well educated with a strong interest in artistic and cultural history.

Venus in the 10th House

Here there is both social and artistic ambition, and if the individual does possess artistic talent, there is a strong likelihood of achieving recognition and success. Marriage will probably be sought with someone who can bestow wealth and status. Relationships with employers will generally be good, and Venus in this house grants success in dealings with the opposite sex, who will help in advancing his or her career. If Venus is afflicted, these individuals can be inclined to forget their old friends as they climb the social and professional ladder.

Venus in the 11th House

Friendships and other relationships resulting from participation in group activities are indicated by Venus in the 11th House. Kindness shown will mean kindness received, adding greatly to the likeliness of hopes and ambitions being realized. Many friendships will be made with members of the opposite sex. Friends can become romantic partners, and romantic partners, friends.

Venus in the 12th House

The 12th-House Venus person loves quiet and solitude, and personal and even social contacts will tend to be secretive or at least of a highly private nature. This also applies to love affairs. But these people's shyness can result in loneliness and unrequited love. Artistic inspiration can come from being deeply attuned to the unconscious mind, and these people are also highly sympathetic and compassionate toward others. They can be extremely sensitive and easily hurt.

ASPECTS OF VENUS

Aspects of Venus, along with the sign it is in and the houses it rules (those where Taurus and Libra are found), show the areas of life most influenced by the need and desire for companionship, how love is expressed on an intimate basis, aesthetic sensibilities, and artistically creative abilities. Venus aspects also indicate whether the individual excels or has difficulty in relating to others, where and how they express social, romantic, and sexual urges, and where they serve and give with love and joy. In a male horoscope, Venus and the factors affecting it indicate the kind of woman he wishes to attract; in a female horoscope, they show what kind of woman she will be for a man.

Venus Conjunctions

Conjunctions of Venus indicate a gentle and graceful expression of the individual's social, romantic, and aesthetic attributes. These individuals have a great deal of emotional sensitivity, and the grace and ease with which they express themselves is especially attractive to the opposite sex. This applies to all areas ruled by the planet or planets that Venus conjuncts in the signs and houses where the conjunction is formed and in the houses and signs ruled by Venus.

Venus Sextiles

Venus sextiles indicate opportunities for social and aesthetic development in the areas ruled by the planets, houses, and signs that form the sextile. Emotional and artistic expression can be refined and affections developed in the areas ruled by the signs and houses which Venus and the planets forming the sextile occupy and rule.

Venus Squares

Venus squares point to either difficulties or more than the "fair dose" of energy in both social and romantic relationships. The affairs ruled by the planets that square Venus and the signs and houses occupied and ruled by these planets will all in some way be affected by this energy.

Venus Trines

Venus trines indicate beauty and grace along with social popularity and happiness in love and romance. The individual benefits greatly from the good will of other people. This will be especially true in the areas affected by the planets that make up the trine and the signs and houses the planets and Venus occupy and rule.

Venus Oppositions

Venus oppositions are a strong indicator of emotional problems and conflicts in marriage and romantic relationships. The individuals tend to be overly sensitive and demanding while giving little in return. Disappointments and unhappiness are the inevitable result. The signs and the houses occupied and ruled by Venus and the opposing planets and the affairs ruled by these planets indicate the areas which will be most affected by this configuration.

CHAPTER 9

MARS

Mars is very important in the horoscope not only due to its link with the Ascendant through its natural rulership of the 1st House, but to its signification of what makes us get up and go.

MARS IN THE SIGNS

In the signs, Mars tells us about how we channel our drives, including what we do to get the things we want, how we assert ourselves with others, and the kind of physical and sexual energy we carry.

Mars in Aries

Mars in Aries indicates uncontainable energy that must find an outlet in which to channel its intense initiative, courage, and impulsiveness. There is a strong drive to get things done, with a great desire to be first. Staying power and sustained enthusiasm, however, may be lacking, so that projects are not seen through to their conclusion. These individuals can be headstrong and extremely independent, with little to no tolerance for opposition or interference. They are highly competitive and enjoy pitting their strength and courage against others, in sports as well as in the game of life in general. They are prone to head injuries and, when sick, run high fevers that would normally kill others but which they somehow survive. If Mars is afflicted here, these people can be fraught with aggressiveness, egotism, impatience, and anger. Although the Mars in Aries temper is violent, such outbursts tend to be short lived. These individuals may also have an unconscious need to prove their worth through outward expressions of strength or courage.

Mars in Taurus

Mars in Taurus produces a strong desire for money and material possessions, with much energy and focus channeled into the practical means for acquiring them. These people may tend to be slow to act but have great determination and perseverance once action is taken and, although not particularly aggressive, can be stubborn and unyielding if challenged. Gifted with patience and precision, they often make good craftsmen and artisans who create objects of beauty and durability out of solid and sturdy materials. If Mars is afflicted, these people can be preoccupied with sex and sensuality as well as with money and material possessions. They can be jealous and possessive. The violence that can arise out of their sexual jealousy can be just as intense as that of Mars in Scorpio (Taurus's opposite).

Mars in Gemini

Mars in Gemini makes for highly active and critical minds, with a love of debate and mental contest, and tends to imbue some sort of mechanical or manual skill. Restlessness is also characteristic of this position, implying that there will be many changes of occupation or working at more than one job at the same time. Ingenuity and resourcefulness are typical characteristics. If Mars is afflicted here, the individual can be argumentative, irritable, sarcastic, abrasive, and rude.

Mars in Cancer

There is a strong tendency here for the individual to be intensely emotional. Moodiness and aggressive anger can be the cause of discord and strife in domestic relationships, and troubled relationships with parents can lead to psychological problems later in life. Suppressed emotions can also lead to psychological ailments, along with ulcers and other stomach problems. These people will have a strong desire to dominate the domestic scene and to own or build their own home, which also makes them very good carpenters and do-it-yourself handypersons.

Mars in Leo

Mars in Leo bestows great energy, willpower, creativity, and charisma, and much of it will be expressed dramatically through the arts. Many actors have Mars in Leo. Mars in this sign instills self-confidence and social flare, making for natural leaders whom others admire. Proud and high-spirited, they have a strong desire to be in the forefront or the limelight.

Their beliefs and opinions are strong and unswerving, which can often inspire opposition from others rather than conversion. The Mars in Leo desires are fixed and passionate, making for individuals who are ardent in their love but also capable of intense jealousy and possessiveness. There is a very strong attraction to the opposite sex, who respond in kind to Mars's vitality. As with Mars in Aries, men with Mars in Leo are inclined to premature boldness. When Mars is afflicted in Leo, an overblown ego, overbearing manner, and a need to dominate others may be evident in the individual.

Mars in Virgo

Mars here indicates great skill and energy, precision, and methodology in whatever work the individual performs. His or her actions are systematically planned and carefully executed. Virgo is the sign of health, and Mars rules sharp instruments, so that quite often surgeons have Mars in this sign. There is a strong tendency toward perfectionism, which can make these subjects overly fastidious. If Mars is afflicted, the individual may have an irritable and nervous temperament, disagreements with employers and coworkers, and/or be at risk of job-related accidents.

Mars in Libra

Libra gives grace and refinement to the otherwise selfish and aggressive tendencies of Mars, and their combined energies gives the individual a strong urge for balanced action within a social context. Libra is a cardinal sign concerned with social relationships and partnerships, so those with Mars in this sign tend to be initiators of social activities. They have a strong desire to be noticed and appreciated by others. Although Mars is here softened and tempered by Venus, these individuals can become very angry when their sense of justice is violated. They seek marriage with an energetic and aggressive partner for the emotional gratification it can provide. If this Mars is afflicted, they can be overly strict concerning the rules of social conduct, and difficulties in partnerships and relationships can arise from conflicts of will.

Mars in Scorpio

Mars in Scorpio confers powerful desires and emotions along with relentless courage and drive. It can represent the heights of spiritual development and achievement or the lowest depths of moral degradation. With steadfast courage, determination, and resourcefulness, Mars in Scorpio will rise to the occasion in the face of adversity. These individuals are capable of an uncompromising fight to the death in defense of their principles. In fact, death will be faced fearlessly if it is necessary to do so in order to accomplish high-minded goals. The powerful sex drive of Mars in Scorpio makes for ardent lovers who are also capable of intense jealousy and possessiveness. These people can be uncompromising, with an all-or-nothing attitude, and prone to making either devoted friends or enemies in their dealings with others. When Mars is afflicted, they can be prone to anger and resentment. Slights and offenses are not easily forgotten and grudges can be held for a long time, making the Mars in Scorpio person a dangerous enemy to have. They may also have a tendency to emotionally dominate others.

Mars in Sagittarius

Mars here dispenses strong religious and philosophical convictions and ideals, often with strong feelings of patriotism and a crusader mentality in the name of the causes and beliefs the individual adheres to. There is also a love of sports and outdoor activities, and Mars in Sagittarius can confer a very distinct love of hunting (Sagittarius is the sign of the Archer, of Artemis, the Greek goddess of the hunt). They also love all kinds of travel and adventure. Mars in Sagittarius desires to be a leader in law, religion, philosophy or education, but with a tendency to follow traditional or conservative paths and to be self-righteous in this regard. Their love of adventure and desire to attain far-reaching goals can cause people with Mars in Sagittarius to scatter their energies and neglect the practical matters of their immediate surroundings. If Mars is afflicted, they may be querulous, with a pronounced lack of diplomacy in expressing opinions, an inability or refusal to see other points of view, and a neurotic desire for freedom at any cost—a sort of flight mechanism. An afflicted Mars in Sagittarius can also indicate political or religious fanaticism.

Mars in Capricorn

Although less sensual than Mars in Taurus or Scorpio, Mars in Capricorn people can be extremely materialistic and driven almost solely by ambition. Their actions are carefully calculated to achieve concrete results—usually the acquisition of money and power. As with Mars in Virgo, these individuals require a practical and concrete reason for anything they do.

The success they achieve is not necessarily selfish, as it also provides the material needs for their families and other dependents. Generally, Mars in this sign confers a high degree of discipline and self-control, along with great pride in doing a job well. They expect the same discipline and obedience from those under them (as they themselves show to their superiors) and have an acute disdain for laziness and lack of ambition. If Mars is afflicted, there is a dark tendency to use people simply for material or political gain, while completely forsaking human values. Since Capricorn's ruler, Saturn, governs the bones, the afflicted Mars in Capricorn may be prone to fractures.

Mars in Aquarius

Mars in Aquarius demands absolute personal freedom to pursue unconventional courses of action, often having to do with reform of the status quo. There is little regard or respect for traditional views or methods unless they are based on practical logic and experience and have objectively earned due consideration. As a result, those with Mars in Aquarius, unlike those with Mars in Capricorn, do not work well under authoritarian direction. For them, teamwork, rather than individual effort, is far more likely to achieve results, which can be considerable, especially in the fields of science and humanitarian endeavors. These people must be allowed to do things their own way and learn by their own mistakes. There is, naturally, the danger of discarding the old ways simply for the sake of discarding them without having anything new and tangible to replace them with. When Mars is afflicted, this can manifest itself in a destructive way with a desire to overthrow the established order without offering anything to regenerate and improve it. Many revolutions have occurred when Mars was in Aquarius. Those with an afflicted Mars in Aquarius are prone to troubles with blood circulation.

Mars in Pisces

With Mars in Pisces, strong and unfettered emotions can rise up from out of the unconscious, and repressed anger can lead to neurosis and psychosomatic illnesses. There is a strong tendency to harbor unconscious resentments. Excessive emotionalism can diminish self-confidence and inhibit decisive action. This is a particularly weak position, Pisces being a mutable water sign. These people will tend to act secretively in order to avoid direct confrontation with their opposition. There is a strong need for periods of quiet and solitude in order for them to come to terms with their feelings and rejuvenate their energies. If Mars is well aspected, it can enhance artistic or musical expression and be beneficial for those who work in psychology. If heavily afflicted, these people can have a tendency to cry easily and manipulate others by requiring attention for physical or psychological problems.

MARS IN THE HOUSES

Mars in the houses shows those areas of life in which we express our desires and the type of action we must initiate to achieve results. Mars afflicted in the house indicates the types of conflict that we are likely to experience.

Mars in the 1st House

These individuals are robust and muscular, aggressive and out-going, and have an abundance of energy and physical stamina. Ambitious and hardworking, they are capable of reaching great heights of achievement if their courage and strength are matched with intelligence and self-discipline. Their competitive instincts drive them to seek recognition and public acclaim. They insist on absolute freedom of action and will not tolerate any interference. If Mars is afflicted, these people can be rash and impulsive, insensitive to the feelings of others, combative, and prone to fits of violent temper. If Mars is heavily afflicted, they can have a tendency to engage in physical fights. Their impulsiveness can lead to a disregard for personal safety. An indicator of Mars in the 1st House can be a scar on the head or face. These people tend to run high fevers when they are ill and often have red or reddish-colored hair. Men with Mars in the 1st House, like those with Mars in Aries, can be prone to early baldness.

Mars in the 2nd House

Mars in the 2nd House points to the active pursuit of wealth and material possessions. These individuals have good earning abilities but may tend to deplete their resources through impulsive spending. They have a strong desire to own and run their own businesses rather than work for anyone else and are always out to prove their capacity to make money by surpassing the competition. Personal property is extremely important to them, and they will fight to protect it. If Mars is afflicted, they may be excessively materialistic and overly concerned about material values. Covetousness can lead to stealing and other dishonest means to acquire that which is desired.

Mars in the 3rd House

Here, the intellect will be highly active, aggressive, and resourceful, with the ability to think quickly in emergency situations. These people tend to be intellectually assertive in order to both acquire and deliver information. Many newspaper reporters, for example, are likely to have Mars in the 3rd House, and they can also be found working with communications-related machinery or in the transportation industry. If Mars is afflicted, these people can be argumentative and sarcastic, with a tendency to jump to conclusions, impatient with what they consider the stupidity of others, and troubled when dealing with contracts and other agreements.

Mars in the 4th House

This placement predisposes the individual to dominate the domestic scene and direct much energy toward the home in general, including the acquisition of property. If Mars is afflicted, this can lead to family quarrels and, in children, conflict with parents. An afflicted Mars can also indicate property-related troubles, including the danger of fire and theft. If well aspected, it can indicate a person who works hard to improve his or her surroundings, not only on the home front but in terms of environmental and ecological concerns. Those with Mars in this position tend to have strong constitutions and energy that they sustain into old age.

Mars in the 5th House

With Mars in the 5th House, love, pleasure, sex, and romance are actively pursued, and the strong sex drive of these individuals gives an added aggression and urgency to the need for a sex partner. If Mars is afflicted, they may find themselves involved in quarrels about sexual jealousy during courtship. A heavily afflicted Mars can mean that sexual passion results in pregnancy out of wedlock, as well as the possibility of the individual's children being subject to accidents or even death. Mars in the 5th House is often found in the horoscopes of athletes, for it conveys a natural love of competitive sports of all kinds. It can also entail a fondness for working with children, and often these people make good teachers who inspire enthusiasm and devotion in their students. If Mars is afflicted, they can be dictatorial and authoritarian to those in their charge.

Mars in the 6th House

Mars in the 6th House makes for hard and energetic workers, with little to no patience for those who are lazy or apathetic. Often, the work done will involve sharp tools or machinery that consumes a large amount of power; thus Mars in this position is often found in the horoscopes of mechanics, engineers, and heavy equipment operators, as well as surgeons and even chefs. Great skill and precision is shown in work, with personal esteem being derived from a job well done. If Mars is afflicted, irritability, ill heath, or job related injuries can result from overwork. Labor disputes and on-the-job conflicts can also arise. Perfectionism and fussiness with details can lead to the neglect of major issues and concerns.

Mars in the 7th House

Mars here emphasizes the importance of partnerships or working with the public. Both marriage and business partners are likely to have active and aggressive Martian natures. The individual's overriding preference is to work and act with a partner, and much can be accomplished if Mars is well aspected. If Mars is afflicted, there will be disagreements with associates and conflict and divorce in marriage, along with a tendency to compete rather than cooperate with others.

Mars in the 8th House

This is a powerful position for Mars, the 8th House corresponding to the sign Scorpio, which Mars rules. The individual possesses very strong desires and emotions, along with a powerful sex drive. He or she has great energy and perseverance in accomplishing goals. There may well be an interest in the occult, psychic phenomena, and spiritualism. Mars in the 8th House can indicate an experience of violent death through war, accident, or strife. If Mars is afflicted, sudden or violent death is possible, and a heavily afflicted Mars can indicate criminal tendencies. Actions are often carried out in secret, both for good and bad purposes.

Mars in the 9th House

Here, there will be a strong interest in travel, sports, and social, religious, and philosophical issues and causes. These people are often passionate crusaders in the name of their ideals and beliefs, expressing themselves in terms of action rather than with mere words. If Mars is well aspected, their broad understanding and concern for humanity can inspire genuine reform for the good of all. If Mars is afflicted, they can be fanatical, intolerant, and narrow-minded. These individuals are seekers of adventure and experience, which often leads them to travel to foreign countries and explore the realms of higher learning and philosophy.

Mars in the 10th House

Mars in the 10th House imbues these individuals with a strong desire for power and fame. They are gifted with initiative and executive ability that enables them to achieve practical goals. Highly driven and competitive, they often achieve fame or notoriety in their chosen fields. If Mars is afflicted, they are capable of resorting to underhanded means to obtain power or position, with a complete disregard for human values. A tumultuous fall and scandalous loss of reputation can result when their wrongdoings are almost inevitably exposed.

Mars in the 11th House

The overriding concern and focus here will be friendships and group associations and activities. Often, these friends and associates are instrumental in assisting the individual in achieving business and professional goals. Mechanical ability and inventiveness are characteristic of Mars in this house, as is activity in bringing about social reforms. If Mars is afflicted, there may be discontent with the prevailing social order and an iconoclastic tendency toward revolution merely for its own sake. Disagreements and conflicts with friends and group associations are also likely. Impulsive and reckless behavior in group situations can lead to injury or death either to the individual or his or her companions.

Mars in the 12th House

Desires and actions are here strongly influenced by the unconscious. These individuals tend to be highly secretive about their desires, purposes, and actions. Also, they may have secret sexual involvements. Many of their activities will be carried out in seclusion. Often, they will be found working in large institutions where they can either hide or lose their personal identities. If Mars is afflicted, there can be secret enemies, involvement in clandestine plots, and the harboring of secret animosities. There is also the danger of incarceration in a prison, hospital, or mental institution, sometimes for political reasons.

ASPECTS OF MARS

Aspects of Mars, the sign, house position, and the houses Mars rules, show how the self is expressed through dynamic action, whether positive or negative, and the areas of life that are affected by such action. Mars represents willful desire. An afflicted Mars indicates a bad or violent temper and a tendency to act rashly and precipitously. Martian energy needs to be constructively and purposefully channeled. Favorable aspects from Mercury, Jupiter, and Saturn offer great assistance in this regard. Mercury provides mental clarity and insight; Saturn, discipline and self-control; and Jupiter, beneficence and altruism. In a woman's horoscope, Mars indicates the type of man she will be attracted to. In a man's horoscope, it represents the way he expresses his masculinity in order to attract a woman.

Mars Conjunctions

Mars conjunctions indicate that direct action will be taken in the affairs ruled by the planet or planets forming the conjunction. The consequences will be felt in the areas ruled by the sign and the houses which Mars and the conjuncting planet(s) rule and occupy. Mars confers courage, energy, and leadership and much can be accomplished with this configuration. If the conjunction is afflicted, the action taken can be rash and ill considered, with the inevitable destructive results.

Mars Sextiles

Mars sextiles indicate that energy and willpower will be applied intelligently toward some constructive purpose and that there will be many opportunities to do so. The mental nature of the sextile is implied by Gemini and the 3rd House and Aquarius and the 11th House, which give clear and insightful direction. The opportunities provided lead to experience, which brings wisdom. Obstacles are overcome with courage and initiative, and great progress is made.

Mars Squares

Mars squares mean that the desire for action will be frustrated and hindered. Often this frustration can cause the individual to act rashly, with destructive results. It is important, with this configuration, to learn patience and consideration for others. Saturn's restriction of Mars's energy can actually be utilized intelligently to accomplish much, as a driving ambition is also an attribute of a Mars square. Those areas of life ruled by the planet or planets forming the square, and the affairs ruled by the signs and houses in which the square is found, will be the most profoundly affected.

Mars Trines

Mars trines indicate that the desire for action and the flow of energy is unobstructed, allowing it to be easily directed toward some constructive use. The individual will have a passionate love of life. Both exuberance and accomplishment will be expressed in the affairs ruled by the planet or planets that form the trine and the houses and signs occupied and ruled by Mars.

Mars Oppositions

Mars oppositions mean that the individual will tend to be competitive and combative. Problems will be caused by rash, angry, and aggressive action toward others. On the positive side, the Mars opposition can make the individual capable of firm and energetic action in partnerships once the individual has been forced to come to terms, often as the result of violent conflicts, with the necessity of cooperation if anything is to be accomplished.

CHAPTER 10

JUPITER

J upiter has long been associated with expansiveness: fortune or the manifestation of positive karma, what we
embrace in ideals and beliefs that brings us to a higher
consciousness, and how we reach out to and relate to others.

JUPITER IN THE SIGNS

The sign in which Jupiter is located in the horoscope tells us
about what kinds of moral, philosophical, and religious beliefs
we hold, how we share our gifts with others, and the goodwill
or financial benefits we are likely to receive.

Jupiter in Aries

Jupiter in Aries confers great abilities for leadership and
innovation in art, philosophy, education, and other social,
cultural, and spiritual endeavors. The highest aspect of Aries
is the self manifested as pure creative spirit, the *I am what
am*, the burning bush that does not perish, and Jupiter in this
sign confers great powers of creative and spiritual regenera-

tion along with an acute understanding and respect for it. These individuals have a profound faith in the possibility of personal and social rebirth into a better way of life, of being and becoming. They have great energy and are inspired and inspiring, arousing those around them to confident and enthusiastic action.

Their initiative and inspired religious and philosophical leadership can, however, also make them egotistical and self-important, which can also arouse resentment in others. Their faith, though, gives them the courage to undertake endeavors that others would not dare to attempt. Their positive efforts, even if they do not attain their seemingly unreachable goals, more often than not produce something good that in turn leads to some form of evolutionary development, Jupiter being the planet associated with the principle of growth. When Jupiter is afflicted in Aries, there can be a highly exaggerated sense of self-importance, actions can be rash and impulsive, and carelessness and overconfidence can lead to losses in business and friendship.

Jupiter in Taurus

Jupiter in Taurus indicates the ability to attract wealth, along with an awareness of the correct and beneficial use of money and material resources. Money and material goods are regarded as a form of energy or sustenance that simply flows from one person to the other for the good of all, like the water of life. Those with Jupiter in Taurus need to learn not only generosity but wisdom and discrimination in investing money so that it be used in the most efficient and constructive way. These individuals are concerned with enjoying the good things in life and have a strong desire to share the wealth they naturally accumulate as a matter of principle.

If Jupiter is afflicted, expensive tastes and indulgence can lead to dissipation of resources and physical degeneration. They can become indifferent to and neglectful of the physical needs of others, leading to jealousy and resentment in those less fortunate. In forgetting that honor and prestige lie not in wealth but in what is done with it, the pride and sense of superiority that can come with financial success can lead to their downfall, and extravagance can result in being buried in debt and trouble with creditors.

Jupiter in Gemini

Here is found a broad intellectual understanding and love of philosophy and the ideas that have shaped history, religion, law, and education. These individuals are mentally and physically restless and are prone to much travel and delving into many areas of study. When negative, they can come across as intellectual dilettantes whose knowledge is wide but superficial and lacking in real or practical experience. This theoretical or book knowledge can produce a pretentious intellectual snob. On the more positive side, their multifaceted intellectual activities can produce an acute understanding of social, political, and historical trends. Jupiter in Gemini confers strong abilities in writing, teaching, and lecturing.

Jupiter in Cancer

Jupiter in Cancer often indicates a good family background, not necessarily of wealth or standing, but one in which moral and religious principles, kindness, and generosity are instilled from an early age. Cancer represents the parents, especially the mother, and it is from the parents that such basic values are learned. Those with Jupiter in Cancer seek to establish a secure, comfortable, and friendly home environment for themselves and their loved ones. They are kind and generous to their family and friends. These individuals are imbued with a strong maternal instinct and may be inclined to want to mother everyone. They have a great love of good food and are often good cooks, which can imply a tendency to over-indulge in the name of the palate. They tend to be emotion-ally idealistic, with a true belief in human kindness and honesty. They often receive financial support or inheritance from their parents or other family members and can become wealthy in the later half of their lives. If Jupiter is afflicted, there can be overindulgence in food and material comforts, an unhealthily close tie to parents, oppressive mother-love, and maudlin sentimentality.

Jupiter in Leo

Those with Jupiter in Leo are blessed with abundant energy, strong constitutions, optimism, and self-confidence. Dignified and inspiring leaders, they are benevolent and generous, although they demand admiration and appreciation in return. If Jupiter is afflicted, conceit and egotism can make them vain and arrogant. If positive, there can be great generosity, hon-esty, expansiveness, reliability, and steadfastness. These people like to do things on a lavish or opulent scale. They have a love of grand parties, parades, pageantry, and drama. Radiating warmth, generosity, and affection, their unselfishness can win the admiration and love of others, often enabling them to find fulfillment in romance. Jupiter in Leo can confer honor and prestige that is very much deserved. These people have a natural and genuine love of children. If Jupiter is well aspected, their offspring are likely to achieve honors and distinctions of their own. Jupiter in Leo can give an aptitude for gambling and stock market speculation, along with business success in entertainment, the arts, sports, and education. If Jupiter is afflicted, unwise gambling and speculations can cause financial ruin, and there can be disappointments and losses in love and children.

Jupiter in Virgo

Here, honesty and integrity in work and business can make for congenial relationships with coworkers, employees, and employers. The working conditions they find themselves in are usually pleasant, and they tend to be paid well for their services. Their moral and religious beliefs are based on the concept of service, and often they will be interested in charitable pursuits involving mental and physical health, hospitals, and educational institutions. Ideals are of little value if they do not have practical application, and this basic realism makes them conservative in their social and moral views, similar to Jupiter in Taurus or Capricorn. They zealously demand absolute integrity in every detail and are able to readily distinguish truth from error or falsity. However, their moralistic concern for perfection can suffer from a lack of relative perspective and make mountains out of molehills. Order and cleanliness are extremely important to them, being representative of moral integrity, and they disapprove strongly of sloppiness in dress, work, and housekeeping. Like Venus in Virgo, however, if Jupiter is here afflicted, they can have the opposite reaction. An afflicted Jupiter can also cause unstable employment with a tendency to drift from job to job, laziness, and dissatisfaction with working conditions, employers, and coworkers.

Jupiter in Libra

Jupiter in Libra has an overriding concern for justice and moral principles in partnerships, marriage, friendships, and other close personal relationships. Marriage will tend to be based on shared spiritual values and a sense of cooperation that go beyond sexual attraction. Their religious and moral concepts are based on love and a sense of fair play and social harmony. Social, philosophical, and religious values are influenced by the spouse and close friends, and these individuals equally influence the attitudes of their friends and associates. Their generosity and consideration of others mean they are popular and well liked and enable them to deal well with the public, making them excellent mediators, psychologists, fundraisers, diplomats, and peacemakers. If Jupiter is here afflicted, they can be prone to making moral decisions for others and desire to be all things to all people, resulting in double standards on many issues and promising more than can be delivered in order to gain approval. They can expect too many favors from others and initiate too many close personal ties at any given time, making those with whom they are involved suspect them of disloyalty. This often leads to sexual treachery and betrayal from members of the opposite sex as a result of jealousy and vindictiveness at feeling that the personal consideration that is their due has been ignored. If Jupiter is heavily afflicted in Libra, there may be lawsuits over unfulfilled legal and financial commitments related to business, property, or marriage.

Jupiter in Scorpio

Jupiter in Scorpio suggests strong dealings with joint or corporate finances, insurance, taxes, legacies, and the like. These individuals will also be interested in the occult, the arcane, and mystical aspects of religion, the afterlife, and communication with the spiritual world. They can also be passionate and uncompromising when it comes to religious beliefs and moral standards of conduct, which can sometimes pit them against powerful and bitter enemies. They are prone to acquiring, as if by magic, secret information about the private lives of others and can themselves have friendships or other relationships based on hidden motivations. There is a chance of receiving inheritances as payback for favors rendered. An afflicted Jupiter in Scorpio, however, can indicate legal battles over inheritances, alimony, insurance, taxes, expenditures, and other related matters, and unwise investments in stocks or partnerships can result in financial losses.

Jupiter in Sagittarius

Jupiter in Sagittarius points to a love of philosophy, education, religion, travel, and foreign cultures. These individuals have a strong need for a moral system of some kind that governs personal conduct, relationships, and way of life, be it religious, political, or philosophical. This desire for behavior and attitudes to conform to an objective or impartial set of principles often brings them respect and admiration, even from those who might be considered their enemies. They will often feel compelled to convert others to their way of thinking. They see acceptance of a belief system or moral code as a means of being able to operate within a larger social context in which the rules are understood. They will have a strong interest in the ideas that have shaped history and society.

If Jupiter is afflicted, these people can be narrow-minded, dogmatic, and self-righteous, expecting all to conform to their beliefs and being intolerant of those who don't. Personal egotism masked as religious, national, or racial chauvinism is their unconscious defense mechanism against the unknown or psychologically and socially threatening. If Jupiter is heavily afflicted, these people can have a fanatical and superstitious adherence to dogmatic religious beliefs.

If positively aspected, Jupiter in Sagittarius gives an innate respect for and understanding of other belief systems and an almost prophetic insight into the future.

Jupiter in Capricorn

Here there will be an overriding concern with the so-called letter of the law rather than with its spirit. If well aspected, Jupiter in Capricorn can confer great integrity in moral conduct and business and political ethics, especially in relation to the responsibilities of high office. These people are generally conservative in outlook and often acquire positions of political or economic responsibility in which they tend to show prudence, although they may be somewhat lacking in imagination, innovation, and creativity. They have a strong drive to attain power and status, which can be based on either personal ambition or an acute sense of social responsibility, or a combination of both. Great wealth is often obtained as a result. In their later years, these individuals can often appear as cold and austere personalities, having sacrificed or neglected much of their personal and family lives in the name of their careers and hiding their frustrations and loneliness behind a mask of dignity and reserve. They have an abhorrence of waste and extravagance, and if Jupiter is afflicted, they can be miserly to a ridiculous extreme in certain areas and overly extravagant in others.

Jupiter in Aquarius

Those with Jupiter in Aquarius insist on social, religious, and moral values that are impartial, democratic, and universal. They are open to all of humanity without biases toward class, race, or religion and are intolerant only of intolerance. Tolerance, acceptance, respect, and cooperation are for them the essentials of any social order and interaction. They realize that without differences and variety, the great, beautiful, and complex tapestry of humanity and culture would not be possible. Many social and religious pioneers have Jupiter in Aquarius. If Jupiter is afflicted, these individuals can advocate or practice revolutionary concepts that are impractical or merely iconoclastic; they may be too casual and unreliable in their relationships with others and generally scattered and undisciplined with their energies.

Jupiter in Pisces

Jupiter in Pisces confers emotional depth, understanding, and compassion, along with mystical tendencies and deeply felt religious convictions. There is, however, the danger that others will take advantage of their sympathy, compassion, and generosity, and it is often necessary for Jupiter in Pisces to learn discrimination and that others must, at a certain point, assume responsibility for their own lives and learn their own life lessons. Along with their mystical inclinations, these individuals can have acute psychic abilities and an intuitive perception of spiritual realms that can result in direct experiences of metaphysical realities. If Jupiter is afflicted in Pisces, there is the danger of cultism and "guru-worship" in the name of sublimating the self for a higher purpose as well as to confer personal spiritual or religious status. An afflicted Jupiter can also indicate a parasitic nature that lives off the charity of friends and social institutions.

JUPITER IN THE HOUSES

Jupiter in the houses shows those areas of life in which we express our religious and philosophical concerns. This is the area in which we share our material and spiritual resources, thus receiving good fortune in return. The house placement indicates where that "bread cast upon the waters" reaps its rewards. It shows the realm in which we are at our most expansive, positive, and optimistic.

Jupiter in the 1st House

Jupiter in the 1st House indicates individuals who are optimistic and sociable. They are honest, trustworthy, benevolent, and amicable and therefore tend to be very popular. Their optimism and confidence inspire the same in others. They are dignified in their bearing and manner, especially in their later years. They will manifest strong social, religious, or educational leadership abilities and like to be regarded as authorities within their chosen fields. They have strong religious and moral convictions, often with deep spiritual insight. Generally, they are fortunate throughout their lives. Often, they appear to be blessed by some kind of divine protection or guardian angel, who often appears right at the eleventh hour. If Jupiter is afflicted, they may have a tendency to grow fat in middle or old age as well as self-indulgent, with a highly inflated sense of self-importance.

Jupiter in the 2nd House

Here there is substantial business ability and good fortune regarding money and property. Those with Jupiter in the 2nd House often engage in businesses involving real estate, food, domestic products, fund-raising, publishing, and travel. Other professional pursuits may be related to psychology, education, hospitals, and other similar institutions. If Jupiter is afflicted, money is likely to disappear as fast as it appears, and debts can be incurred due to overreaching and lack of foresight in business dealings.

Jupiter in the 3rd House

Jupiter in the 3rd House makes for congenial relations with siblings and neighbors. These individuals are optimistic and philosophical, with a strong intellectual interest in trends in social thought and communication, especially as expressed in speech and writing. They will also be fond of travel. If Jupiter is afflicted, there can be conflict with siblings and neighbors and, as a result of recklessness, a danger of accidents while traveling.

Jupiter in the 4th House

Jupiter here is an indicator of congenial family relations and domestic comfort and security. These individuals tend to come from families that are financially secure, with good standing in the community, and thus enjoy many social and economic benefits. There will be good fortune in the individual's second half of life, with the likelihood of inheriting property from parents or relatives. If Jupiter is afflicted, family members may become burdens emotionally, or financially, or both.

Jupiter in the 5th House

Here there will be creative involvement in the arts, sports, education, and all aspects of dealing with children. These people have a particular fondness for children, making them good teachers, counselors, and advocates, and their own progeny usually achieve honor and distinction in their own right, having been nurtured well. Jupiter in the 5th House, unless badly afflicted, usually indicates good fortune and happiness in romance, often with someone of wealth or status. Business endeavors can often involve the stock market, investments, the arts, entertainment, or education. Many movie and theatrical producers have Jupiter in the 5th House. An afflicted Jupiter can mean losses resulting from unwise speculations or investments. Like Jupiter in the 2nd House, there is a tendency for these people to overextend themselves and invite financial disaster (brought about, perhaps, by Jupiter's corulership of Pisces, the sign most associated with karma).

Jupiter in the 6th House

With Jupiter in the 6th House, the house associated with Virgo, there will be an active and dedicated interest in service, driven by a desire to serve others and contribute to society in a practical and constructive way. Work related to mental and physical healing can be fulfilling here, for these individuals tend to have an innate understanding of mental and emotional states as they affect physical health. Usually, they are well liked and respected in their work and enjoy congenial relations with coworkers, employees, and employers. If Jupiter is afflicted, the opposite will be the case. If Jupiter is badly afflicted, the individual may be subject to laziness and liver problems due to overindulgence.

Jupiter in the 7th House

Here, openness and friendliness, along with a sound moral sense in relationships with others, often lead to good fortune through marriage and other partnerships. Those with Jupiter in the 7th House have a strong sense of justice; they are fair and honest in their dealings with others and expect the same in return. They often marry someone of wealth or social standing, and their moral and spiritual values regarding relationships often lead to a stable and lasting union. Business partnerships also prove fruitful, owing to good judgment in choosing associates. These people will have strong abilities in the fields of law, public relations, sales, negotiation, and mediation. If Jupiter is afflicted, they may be naive or gullible in partnerships and business dealings, making them easy victims for con artists and opportunistic predators. They can also have a tendency to take too much for granted and expect too much from others.

Jupiter in the 8th House

Jupiter in the 8th House indicates a strong chance of benefits through inheritance, insurance, and joint finances. On the other hand, if Jupiter is afflicted, conflict and litigation involving the same may occur. These individuals are often attracted to businesses involving insurance, taxes, and corporate fundraising. They will have a strong interest in life after death and other matters pertaining to spiritualism. Unless Jupiter is afflicted, these individuals can look forward to a death in later life that is peaceful and brought about by natural causes.

Jupiter in the 9th House

Those with Jupiter in the 9th House have an innate love of philosophy, religion, and higher education. They make excellent teachers and are often associated with institutions of higher learning. If Jupiter is afflicted, they may be hindered in their ability to acquire the education they desire, or they may be lazy and undisciplined or indifferent about the knowledge and qualifications they have attained. Generally, they are broad-minded, learned, and tolerant. If Jupiter is afflicted, they can be narrow-minded, dogmatic, and extremist in their beliefs. These individuals will have a great love of travel and an intense curiosity about foreign cultures.

Jupiter in the 10th House

Jupiter in the 10th House indicates professional achievement, prominence, and acclaim, usually in the later part of life. These people are consummate professionals, known for their personal standards of excellence. Religious and moral principles also govern their business dealings. With Jupiter in this house, the individual has considerable professional ambition, along with honesty and reliability. Developing a highly dignified manner as he or she grows older, this individual is likely to acquire wealth during his or her later years. This is particularly true if Jupiter is in an earth sign. Like Jupiter in Capricorn, the individual's domestic life can suffer as a result of so much time and energy being devoted in the pursuit of a career. If Jupiter is afflicted, hypocrisy and vainglory can lead to downfall and disgrace.

Jupiter in the 11th House

Jupiter in the 11th House achieves its goals through friendships and social relationships based on shared interests and concerns. Favors are rendered and returned, as these people are kind, well liked, and tend to attract friends who are generous and helpful. A spirit of mutual cooperation and consideration enables them to successfully carry out large and constructive enterprises to the benefit of all. Business may relate to social organizations, science, and inventions. If Jupiter is afflicted, the individual's attitudes and goals may be impractical, and friendships may be based on selfish or ulterior motives. There can be a tendency to use people while neglecting one's personal responsibilities toward them.

Jupiter in the 12th House

Here, there is a need for seclusion, solitude, introspection, and meditation in the search for life's spiritual truths. Intuition and mysticism tend to be prevalent with Jupiter in this house.

There is a deep empathy and sympathy for the less fortunate and humanity in general, and these individuals gain emotional satisfaction from helping others. They are natural peacemakers, with the ability to make friends out of enemies. They can often be found working quietly in large institutions like hospitals, asylums, universities, and churches. Humility and sincerity are typical of Jupiter in this house. If Jupiter is afflicted, the individual can suffer from neurosis, a martyr complex, unrealistic idealism, and a tendency to escape into fantasy. The afflicted 12th-House Jupiter person can refuse to take responsibility for his or her own welfare and depend on charitable institutions or the generosity of friends for support, basically becoming a parasite. With a well-aspected Jupiter, the person may tend to receive unexpected aid in times of crisis as karmic payback for his or her own good deeds.

ASPECTS OF JUPITER

Aspects of Jupiter, along with the house, sign position, and the houses Jupiter rules, show how and where individual growth and expansion, in the process of becoming or self-actualization, takes place. With easy aspects, we gain the cooperation of others based on shared social, philosophical, moral, and religious attitudes with the goal of providing for the collective good of society. Jupiter indicates the way in which we give to the collective in order to take from it. The planets aspecting Jupiter indicate how we cooperate and contribute to the greater social structure and serve the general welfare. If Jupiter is afflicted with difficult aspects, we may experience difficulty cooperating with commonly accepted modes of social behavior, or we may need to examine our motives for doing so.

Jupiter Conjunctions

Jupiter conjunctions indicate individuals who are benevolent and generous, imbued with optimism, goodwill, and a constructive awareness of life's possibilities. Thus they readily gain the support and cooperation of others. The affairs ruled by the planets forming the conjunction, and the houses and signs the planets occupy and rule, show where increase and good fortune reside in the individual's life.

Jupiter Sextiles

Jupiter sextiles show that there will be opportunities for mental growth and development regarding the affairs governed by the planets in the sextile, as well as the signs and houses which Jupiter and the planet(s) occupy and rule. These individuals will work well with groups and have good relationships with siblings and neighbors. They will profit through education, travel, writing, and communication in general.

Jupiter Squares

With Jupiter squares, too much ambition can lead to failure as a result of attempting more than can be accomplished. Moderation and careful planning need to be exercised in the affairs ruled by Jupiter and the squaring planets as well as the signs and houses that they occupy and rule.

Jupiter Trines

Jupiter trines point to good fortune, unimpeded progress, and the rewards of past actions, all found, naturally, in the areas of life ruled by the trining planets or planets and the signs and houses that Jupiter and the planet(s) occupy and rule.

Jupiter Oppositions

Jupiter oppositions indicate a tendency to demand too much from others and take too much for granted, resulting in relationship problems involving the planet or planets that oppose Jupiter, and the signs and houses that Jupiter and the planet(s) occupy and rule. The individual's jocular countenance and grandiose schemes will, in the end, not be greeted kindly by those who feel they have paid too high a price to go along with them.

CHAPTER 11

SATURN

The mythology of Saturn, or Cronus, is full of dark symbolism generally associated with the struggle of differentiation involved in becoming a unique yet respected individual. However, if we accept Saturn as the Cosmic Teacher and pay attention to his lessons, we may be better equipped to carry our burdens. Saturn is the strongest indicator of the career path upon which we are likely to embark.

SATURN IN THE SIGNS

Saturn in the signs shows the nature of our responsibilities and the kind of discipline we must achieve in order to work positively within life's limitations, which actually give embodiment and structure to our highest aspirations.

Saturn in Aries

These individuals will be compelled by circumstances to acquire initiative and self-reliance in providing themselves with the practical necessities of life. By being obliged to develop their own resources, they in turn develop strength of will and character. Saturn represents the laws of cause and effect, the consequences of action, and Aries, the primary impulse to action. In Aries, a new cycle of experience is just beginning, and consequences are yet to be felt and their lessons learned. As a result, these individuals may be lacking in sufficient awareness of social justice and the rights of others in terms of the effects of their actions, as well as the effects of those actions upon themselves. On the other hand, Saturn in Aries can provide resourcefulness, initiative, and creativity, enabling these individuals to bring new concepts and innovations to their chosen fields. Albert Einstein is a supreme example of a well-aspected Saturn in Aries. If Saturn is afflicted, these people can be self-centered and defensive, assuming that others are opposed to them and making it difficult for them to communicate and cooperate. Being overly concerned with their own ambition and security, they can tend to overlook the needs and concerns of others. These flaws can impose strong limitations on their success. They like to do things alone without asking for or relying on the assistance of others. Saturn in Aries can cause a tendency to worry and headaches resulting from a restriction of the blood flow to the brain.

Saturn in Taurus

With Saturn in Taurus, these individuals have a strong need for financial and emotional security. Material possessions, upon which their sense of security is often based, are only acquired through discipline and hard work. A well-aspected Saturn bestows patience, endurance, practicality, and an adherence to principles. At around the age of twenty-nine or thirty, these individuals will seek financial and domestic stability, which their sense of well-being depends upon. They often enter such professions as banking, business management, and insurance. If Saturn is afflicted, they can be excessively materialistic, obstinate, and miserly.

Saturn in Gemini

With Saturn in Gemini, the first air sign and the sign concerned with the form and function of communication, we meet a mind that is logical, well disciplined, and practical. These people possess a great reasoning ability to solve problems and express ideas verbally and in writing. They judge ideas according to their practicality and proven value. Saturn in Gemini individuals like things to be clearly defined down to the last detail, and this is particularly true when it comes to contracts and agreements. Honesty in communication and dependability are of utmost importance to them. They are disciplined in all forms of mental activity and often excel in science and mathematics—indeed, in any work requiring the concrete implementation or expression of ideas. They are adaptable to the practical needs of any situation. If Saturn is afflicted, these individuals can display excessive doubt, suspicion, and shyness and can tend to be overly analytical and critical.

Saturn in Cancer

Saturn in Cancer can cause repression of emotional expression and estrangement from family members, resulting in emotional and psychological isolation. Early relationships with parents and siblings are often cold and problematic, leaving emotional scars that cause inhibitions and neurotic tendencies, although these individuals still remain devoted to their families and take their responsibilities toward them very seriously. Saturn in Cancer is often an indicator of domestic instability and insecurity. The need for respect for both the individual and the family is felt deeply by these individuals, and they often hide their emotions in order to preserve their dignity. The resulting armor in which they encase themselves can cause difficulties in close personal relationships. A poor digestion and sluggish metabolism can cause some of them to be overweight, while others may appear thin and undernourished. An afflicted Saturn in Cancer can also result in hypersensitivity and a strong attachment to material possessions.

Saturn in Leo

Saturn in Leo gives a strong desire for power and leadership. These people have an almost compulsive need to personally control their environment, and if Saturn is afflicted, they can be dictatorial and dogmatic. They require the recognition and respect of others and can be very demanding of attention. Security is sought through autocratic means. Parents with Saturn in Leo are usually strict and severe disciplinarians when it comes to their children. These individuals need to set aside their egos and develop a proper attitude toward love, romance, friendship, children, and self-expression. Professionally, they may be interested in education and business management, which can involve the entertainment industry. An afflicted Saturn can cause disappointments in love and problems with children, along with financial losses resulting from poor speculation. Heart trouble and back problems, especially stiff muscles, are physical ailments related to Saturn in Leo.

Saturn in Virgo

Here we have individuals who are extremely practical, hardworking, and exacting in their concern for efficiency, detail, precision, and accuracy. If Saturn is afflicted, suffice it to say that perfectionism can be taken to a dysfunctional extreme and have a negative effect on relations with coworkers, employees, and employers. These people are often found working in such fields as health and medicine, scientific research, and detailed record-keeping professions like accounting and library science. Often, they can appear to be austere and depressed owing to the weight and responsibility of their work. It is important that they learn to relax, develop a sense of humor, and enjoy themselves once in a while. Worry and overwork can result in illness, especially ailments related to nervousness and digestion.

Saturn in Libra

Libra is the sign that rules relationships, and Saturn in Libra indicates a strong concern with the responsibilities and rules thereof and contracts between people, both in marriage and business. Saturn in Libra recognizes that mutual agreement, cooperation, commitment, and justice are essential to creating enduring human relationships, whether it be marriage, business, or close friendships. Since Saturn in Libra rules contracts, these agreements are often of a karmic nature, based on past debts and responsibilities. Saturn in Libra may indicate marriage in later life or marriage to an individual with serious business or professional obligations. Those with Saturn in this sign are often lawyers, judges, and mediators. If Saturn is afflicted, these people may have exacting attitudes toward others, with a tendency to strictly apply the letter of the law rather than understanding its spirit. They may lack love, forgiveness, and a sense of responsibility in their relationships. Alternatively, they can be inclined to make too many commitments, resulting in overwork or an inability to make good on their promises.

Saturn in Scorpio

Saturn in Scorpio indicates heavy responsibility in dealing with financial affairs, especially the finances and property of others, which can include corporate resources, a partner's finances, taxes, inheritance, and insurance. These individuals tend toward perfectionism in their work and can be hard taskmasters both on themselves and others, with no patience for laziness or lack of diligence. Much energy and discipline will be exerted in the name of achieving practical goals. Responsibilities are taken on with a serious steadfastness. Persistence, thoroughness, and a grim determination are characteristic of Saturn in Scorpio. The will to power and authority is very strong, and these people will struggle hard to realize their ambitions, whether the means is fair or foul, depending on how Saturn is aspected.

When Saturn is afflicted, conflict over joint finances, inheritance, and taxes may arise, resulting in litigation and loss. There can also be a tendency to scheme and plot in secret, with a deep desire for revenge and an inability or refusal to forgive and forget. Saturn in Scorpio people can harbor deep resentment if they feel unjustly done by and possess a fanatic adherence to principles. Health problems from constipation and calcification may arise.

Saturn in Sagittarius

Saturn in Sagittarius describes people who have strict moral codes or a rigid adherence to religious principles. They will be intently serious in their pursuit of philosophy, religion, and higher education in their search for the truth and constructive values that guide personal behavior. In this sense, they are highly moral, be they enlightened or misguided. They have a fierce intellectual pride and a deep need for the kind of intellectual, philosophical, or spiritual achievement that brings distinction and recognition. Their personal reputations are extremely important to them, and they have an acute fear of disapproval and criticism of any sort. With an afflicted Saturn, they can be self-righteous, dogmatic, and imperious in imposing their beliefs and values on others.

Saturn in Capricorn

Here there will be a strong ambition to achieve worldly power, status, and authority. These individuals are possessed by a driving need to make significant achievements in their careers. Whatever endeavors they undertake will have a practical purpose and reward. However, they are not risk takers. They will protect their security while pursuing their ambitions, gaining the prominence they desire without putting either in jeopardy. Thus, they tend to be conservative in both business and politics and obedient to their superiors, and expect the same obedience when they themselves gain positions of authority. Their own early struggles in life make them believe that everyone should earn what he or she gets through personal effort and that only practical experience and hard work can qualify anyone to advise others or take on the responsibilities of power. In this sense, they tend to be basically right, although sometimes too severe, although they often make good mentors. Here is the knowledge that everything in life has its price and that one must give something back to the world in order to take from it. When they do reach positions of power, they take it upon themselves to teach others to help themselves. If Saturn is afflicted, they can use their wealth and power to control others, and may, in later life, forget the struggles of their own youth and be harsh and unsympathetic toward those who are embarking without adequate resources but whose ambition, talent, sincerity, and willingness to work are apparent. As with Saturn in Scorpio, these individuals are capable of reaching the heights of spiritual awareness or descending into the unfulfilling depths of materialism, selfishness, baseness, and callousness toward those less fortunate than themselves. Generally, they are imbued with a strong sense of family pride. They often come from well-to-do families of high standing. In such cases, there is a danger, owing to the lack of any knowledge of life's struggles, to regard their social and economic inferiors with a certain cold disdain, as merely objects to be manipulated and used. If, on the other hand, they have lived through a childhood of poverty and deprivation, Saturn in Capricorn can provide the drive to overcome difficulties and achieve success and social status. If Saturn is well aspected, they will engage their integrity and honesty in all their dealings. If afflicted, unscrupulous means are likely to be employed to achieve selfish goals, resulting in public disgrace and a fall from power. There is also a danger of being too rigid in attitudes and beliefs.

Saturn in Aquarius

Saturn in Aquarius signifies a mind that is impersonal and scientific, with a paramount concern for the truth in all matters. Here, the ego can be set aside to see all issues in the light of objectivity and universal law. These individuals will possess great powers of mental concentration. They are intellectually ambitious as well as original, often working hard to make some scientific breakthrough or discovery. They possess the ability to visualize form and structure, often of a geometrical nature, and are gifted mathematically. Like Saturn in Libra, Saturn in Aquarius confers an acute sense of justice and responsibility in relationships, making these individuals loyal to both the friends and groups with whom they work. If Saturn is afflicted, they can be domineering and selfish, using others to serve their own personal interests. They can also exhibit coldness and emotional insensitivity in personal relationships. The individual's manner can be formal, aloof, and exclusive, with an excessive intellectual pride.

Saturn in Pisces

Here we have the karmic planet in the karmic sign. These individuals have a strong tendency to become trapped in their memories of the past. A fearful and overactive imagination can create anxieties and neuroses of all types, imagining slights and problems where none actually exist, and it can become difficult to deal effectively with the demands of the present. On the other hand, Saturn in Pisces can confer a deep emotional understanding, a strong sense of altruism, and the willingness to work hard in the name of helping the less fortunate. Humility and psychological insight into others, along with a profound spirituality, can be Saturn in Pisces' special gift. If Saturn is afflicted, these individuals can suffer from paranoia, excessive worry, and anxiety and regret arising from being haunted by past mistakes and misfortunes. When taken to the extreme, these tendencies can result in psychosis. Neurosis can cause physical illness. When these people are able to master their psyches, realizing both their strengths and weaknesses, they can overcome their difficulties, let go of the past, and act creatively and constructively on the present, often with startling results. Their work is most likely to be done quietly and behind the scenes in large institutions such as universities, hospitals, and the like.

SATURN IN THE HOUSES

Saturn in the houses shows those areas in our life in which we must acquire and exercise discipline in order to carry our burdens. Here are the practical circumstances that require maturity and personal responsibility, and where ambition will be expressed, and challenges and obstacles met and overcome.

Saturn in the 1st House

Saturn in the 1st House makes for individuals who are serious-minded and hardworking, accepting personal responsibility and tending to neither speak nor act without definite purpose. Although they have a dignified manner, they can also appear to be cold, austere, and unfriendly to the casual observer. However, they are grateful and loyal to those friends who provide them with assistance when it is needed, and they have a strong sense of justice based on pragmatic reasoning. Often, the feeling that they must shoulder heavy responsibilities can result in a lack of humor and personal enjoyment, deeming such things as frivolous and wasteful. If Saturn is afflicted, childhood hardships and deprivations can mean that many obstacles have to be overcome before self-sufficiency and independence are obtained. Childhood suffering and the subsequent psychological wounds can result in a protective mistrust of others and a selfish and materialistic ambition in the name of self-preservation. This creates a defensive shield that becomes difficult for others to penetrate. The sense of loneliness and alienation is thus further enhanced in a vicious cycle of cause and effect.

These individuals will work long and hard to achieve success and power. However, limitations on the fulfillment of their ambitions can cause a hidden hostility and resentment, making them prone to covert scheming in order to exact revenge and take advantage of others. The lesson of Saturn in the 1st House is to learn to love, trust, and cooperate with others. Then, success and fulfillment will be achieved. An afflicted Saturn here can lead to physical disabilities or hardships. Also, two distinct physical types can result from this placement, one short with a dark complexion, the other tall and big boned.

Saturn in the 2nd House

Great ambition and hard work to acquire money, material possessions, and status are characteristic of Saturn in the 2nd House. Generally, these individuals will have to work hard to achieve their goals, but they are shrewd in their business dealings and able to store away their money. Caution and frugality, though, can result in stinginess, which can hinder business expansion and mean that opportunities are lost. Often, their cautiousness is the result of a deep-rooted fear of poverty. They need to learn to be more fluid in their business dealings, that to make money, money must also be spent and risks taken. If Saturn is afflicted, much hard work can result in little to no gain. A well-aspected Saturn can bring financial security and the easy acquisition of wealth, particularly in the later years. Material gain through the father, an employer, or people in powerful positions is also a distinct possibility.

Saturn in the 3rd House

Saturn gives patience and methodology to the thinking processes, and here there will be great mental discipline and practicality through which ideas are judged according to their useful application. A 3rd-House Saturn person's speech will be slow and deliberate, and scientific and mathematical abilities apparent. Those with Saturn in this house are often found working in publishing, printing, and other communications media. They make good accountants, researchers, librarians, writers, and teachers. They are always careful with agreements and wary and thorough when it comes to signing contracts. An afflicted Saturn can mean troubles with siblings and neighbors. It can also cause worry, negative thinking, and difficulties in obtaining the desired education. A well-aspected Saturn means that much diligence and hard work will go into acquiring the right education or training for career purposes.

Saturn in the 4th House

With Saturn in the 4th House many burdens and responsibilities will be incurred through the home and family. The parents are likely to be strict and conservative and may themselves be a burden in their later years. Saturn in this house can mean emotional isolation from the family. These individuals often have to struggle hard to provide for their families and achieve financial and domestic security. Professional and business interests often revolve around real estate, building, farming, or the manufacture of domestic goods. Care must be taken in managing the home, property, and inheritance. These people may become shut-ins or recluses in later life or be restricted to their homes by force of circumstance.

Saturn in the 5th House

Saturn in the 5th House often indicates heavy burdens and responsibilities concerning children. In a woman's horoscope, it can indicate difficulties with childbirth. Romantic involvements generally entail burdensome obligations, and these people often become involved with older, mature partners. A well-aspected Saturn in the 5th House can bestow a desire for power and leadership through artistic self-expression. Business and politics can also provide creative outlets. These people can make good investors and stockbrokers.

If Saturn is afflicted in the 5th House, the individual may experience disappointments in love or a distinct lack of romantic opportunities owing to too much self-conscious reserve and an inability to reach out warmly to others. Only when Saturn in the 5th House learns to express love openly will happiness and fulfillment be attained. If Saturn is heavily afflicted, there can be an inability to relate to children and a tendency to be too stern and strict with them. Emotional coldness and blockages can also cause sexual inhibitions and frigidity.

Saturn in the 6th House

Here, heavy responsibilities will be incurred through work or service. An ability to work hard and efficiently is also indicated, with work taken very seriously and requiring some sort of specialized skill. There is also a serious attitude toward health and hygiene. Mercury's rulership of the 6th House bestows a carefully analytic mind. These individuals are inclined toward careers in medicine, science, engineering, and other fields that require skill and precision. A well-aspected Saturn means that they will be respected by their employers, employees, and coworkers. If Saturn is afflicted, there can be chronic health problems and low vitality as a result of overwork and worry, and work relationships can be strained and stressful.

Saturn in the 7th House

The 7th House corresponds to Libra, the sign in which Saturn is exalted, thus conferring a strong sense of justice and responsibility in all important relationships and transactions. These people tend to either marry late in life or marry a mature, serious-minded and career-oriented individual. If Saturn is well aspected, the marriage will be stable and long lasting. If afflicted, marriage and partnerships will be problematic. Those with Saturn in the 7th House are capable of working hard and responsibly in cooperation with others, upholding their side of all agreements. They have a keen interest in law and are skilled in formulating contracts and in business management. If Saturn is afflicted, they can be critical and inhibited in their relationships, and their marriage partner may be cold, critical, interfering, and unloving. An afflicted Saturn can indicate treacherous enemies and lawsuits. Saturn in the 7th House means that these individuals often find themselves forced into relationships that entail burdens and responsibilities.

Saturn in the 8th House

Saturn in the 8th House, which corresponds to Scorpio, indicates involvement with partners' resources and finances, and the subsequent responsibility this involvement naturally entails in terms of being accountable for other people's money and property. An afflicted Saturn can mean litigation, losses, and other troubles involving other people's money and property. Death may be caused from long-term illness. Disturbing dreams and psychic experiences that have a detrimental psychological effect are common with this placement. Marriage may entail a financial burden, and there may be restrictions on fulfilling career ambitions due to lack of income or capital. If Saturn is well aspected, money can be made through skillful management of a partner's resources, and the individual can attain deep spiritual insight into the meaning of life's mysteries.

Saturn in the 9th House

Saturn in the 9th House points to a serious interest in religion, philosophy, and higher education, with a concern for their practical value in governing action and behavior and contributing to the betterment and stability of society. Education, especially at some acclaimed institute of higher learning, will be sought for the status and professional advancement it can bring. As with Saturn in Sagittarius, these individuals seek personal distinction in the areas of religion, education, and philosophy and desire power and authority within the institutions that govern these fields. Religious and moral standards tend to be conservative, and they are extremely concerned with their moral reputation. If Saturn is afflicted, they can be narrow-minded, rigid, and authoritarian in their attitudes and views.

Saturn in the 10th House

The 10th House corresponds to Capricorn, which Saturn rules, so this strong placement indicates great ambition and an enormous drive to achieve professional status and success. This will become paramount after the age of twenty-nine. A well-aspected Saturn means that hard work and integrity will bestow power, authority, and wealth, especially in later life. Farsighted organizational and managerial abilities are indicated. A well-aspected Saturn in the 10th House is very favorable for politicians and executives. An afflicted Saturn can mean that obstacles, lack of opportunity, and just bad luck can stand in the way of achieving success. A tendency to compromise principles in the name of blind ambition can lead to reversals of fortune and public disgrace.

Saturn in the 11th House

Great care, consideration, and responsibility in relationships with others, both personal friendships and group associations, are indicative of Saturn in the 11th House. Important and influential individuals will be sought out as a means of advancing the individual's career and status, and with friends they will enjoy an equal exchange of loyalty and good advice. Shared interests will provide opportunities to gain knowledge and grow intellectually. If Saturn is afflicted, the individual and his or her friends and associates may use each other for personal gain. A well-aspected Saturn means that the individual holds a sense of equal justice for all in his or her friendships and group associations, from which everybody benefits. Often these friendships and associations are karmic in nature. There is a strong likelihood of friendships with older individuals who provide wisdom and guidance as well as opportunities for advancement.

Saturn in the 12th House

Saturn in the 12th House often means that recognition will be hard to obtain, unless Saturn is favorably aspected to the 10th House or its planetary ruler. These individuals will probably spend much time in seclusion or working quietly behind the scenes in some large institution. An afflicted Saturn here, however, can impart loneliness and depression. If badly afflicted, it can indicate mental illness and confinement in a hospital or prison. Often, it indicates secret enemies who are instrumental in the individual's downfall, although in many cases these enemies may be more imaginary than real. A well-aspected Saturn in the 12th House means that these individuals can escape their psychological problems by working vigorously and serving others in a constructive way that energizes them and gives them a greater purpose.

ASPECTS OF SATURN

Aspects of Saturn, as well as the house, sign position, and the houses it rules (the 10th House and those in which Capricorn and Aquarius are found in the natal chart), indicate our capacity for self-discipline and how and where we will apply it to structuring our life. Saturn's placement and aspects to other planets show where we will be compelled to fulfill ourselves and correct the mistakes of the past, thus acquiring experience, wisdom, and redemption. Without a well-placed Saturn, progress in life can be a struggle, as the discipline and experience necessary to accomplish anything worthwhile are lacking or hard to come by. An afflicted Saturn can make us feel we're prisoner of our personal limitations rather than inspiring us to work constructively with them. Misfortune is often the result. A well-placed Saturn confers strong ambition and a desire to create something of lasting value.

Saturn Conjunctions

Saturn conjunctions indicate ambition and hard work, along with obstacles and limitations that must be overcome. These individuals tend to be conservative, serious, and highly disciplined. Their austere natures are often an impediment to warm or close relationships. These characteristics will be most evident in the affairs ruled by the planet or planets forming the conjunction and the signs and houses Saturn and the planet(s) rule and occupy.

Saturn Sextiles

Saturn sextiles indicate that progress and mental growth and development will be achieved through hard work and good organization and planning. These individuals will be loyal to family, friends, neighbors, employers, and employees. These influences will be most evident in the affairs governed by the signs and houses which Saturn and the planet(s) forming the sextile rule and occupy.

Saturn Squares

Saturn squares indicate severe obstacles and limitations imposed on the individual's ambitions and quest for happiness. These people are fated to work twice as hard to achieve the results others attain with relative ease. Saturn squares indicate major life problems to be overcome, but they can also be a Job-like source of inspiration that drives the individual to greater achievement. These difficulties and obstacles will be found in the affairs ruled by the squaring planet or planets, and the signs and houses which Saturn and the planet(s) occupy and rule.

Saturn Trines

Trines of Saturn indicate that creative discipline and philosophical insight bring good fortune and success in those affairs and arenas governed by the planets that form the trine and are governed by the signs and houses that Saturn and the planet(s) rule and occupy. High moral conduct and standards inspire the confidence and trust of others, granting these individuals positions of authority and responsibility.

Saturn Oppositions

Oppositions of Saturn point to relationship problems that are the result of selfish, negative, and restrictive attitudes toward others. This will be felt most strongly in the affairs ruled by the planet or planets opposing Saturn and the signs and houses that Saturn and the planet(s) rule and occupy. Dour and austere, these individuals often seem unfriendly and unapproachable, which only serves to enhance their feelings of loneliness and alienation, characteristics they must learn to correct if happiness is to be attained.

CHAPTER 12

URANUS

Uranus is the first of the transpersonal planets, spending roughly seven years in one sign of the Zodiac. It is the planet of intuition, sudden and innovative insight, and the urge toward freedom.

URANUS IN THE SIGNS

Because of its slow movement, large groups of people have Uranus in the same sign, which tends to speak of demographic dynamics. The more personal effects of Uranus are indicated by its placement in the houses and the aspects it forms with the other planets in the horoscope.

Uranus in Aries

Freedom of action is of paramount importance to those born with Uranus in Aries. Courageous, daring, and resourceful, they are groundbreaking pioneers in science and social reform. Suffice it to say that they see this as their mission in life. Blunt and outspoken, this generation demands change and the adoption of new lifestyles. They have a strong spirit of adventure and are in constant search of new experiences. When Uranus is afflicted, these individuals can be explosive, impulsive, violent, politically fanatical, and indiscriminate and iconoclastic in their rejection of the past. People who were born between 1928 and 1934 have Uranus in Aries square Pluto in Cancer. Impulsiveness, temperamental and egotistical violence, and blind and aggressive individualism are the pitfalls of Uranus in Aries.

Uranus in Taurus

Those born with Uranus in Taurus have new and innovative ideas about the use of money and resources and often seek economic reform based on humanitarian principles. They are endowed with a strong sense of purpose and determination. As a result, if Uranus is afflicted, they can be stubborn and unyielding. Uranus's urge to freedom and self-expression is limited by Taurus's materialism and attachments to home and family. A well-aspected Uranus in Taurus can bestow considerable artistic talents, especially in music, and these people are often interested in the use of electronics in business and management.

Uranus in Gemini

The generation with Uranus in Gemini is gifted with brilliant and intuitive minds; they are the progenitors of new ways of thinking, pioneers in science, literature, education, and communication. They can, however, be prone to an extreme restlessness that can make it difficult for them to bring things to completion. Self-discipline is necessary for the concrete fruition of their ideas. Given their restlessness and curiosity, they tend to travel a great deal, meeting new people and discovering new ideas. If Uranus is afflicted in Gemini, thinking can be disjointed, scattered, and impractical. There can be conflicted or unreliable relationships with siblings and neighbors, and travel can be beset by confusion and even danger as a result of accidents.

Uranus in Cancer

Those born between June 1949 and June 1956 have Uranus in Cancer. They seek freedom and excitement through emotional expression and independence from the restrictions of family life and parental authority. They desire an egalitarian relationship with their parents and try to make them less their parents and more their friends. This is very much the relationship between the generation known as the baby boomers and their parents who went through WWII. Upon leaving home, these people make sure they will be able to return if the new worlds they are exploring prove to be unsatisfactory, hostile, or unworkable. They may tend to have an interest in communal living or in untraditional ideas of family. They see their homes as gathering places for friends and group activities. In a way, it may be said they have a strong, nomadic tribal sensibility, wishing to share the comforts of their fire, food, and tent with their like-minded fellow travelers. Often their friends become part of their extended family. Uranus in Cancer bestows considerable psychic sensitivity. An afflicted Uranus can cause an erratic and unpredictable temperament.

Uranus in Leo

People born with Uranus in Leo seek freedom in love and romance. They have untraditional ideas and morals about courtship and sex and are likely to be advocates of free love. They are born innovators, with strong willpower and creativity and are capable of developing new concepts in art, theater, and music. They refuse to conform to the standards of society, and instead create and live by their own rules. If Uranus is afflicted, there is a danger of excessive pride and egotism. They can be stubborn and unyielding, incapable of compromise and cooperation with others, insisting on going their own way at any cost.

Uranus in Virgo

Virgo is ruled by Mercury, the planet of communication, knowledge, and scientific thought (Mercury was the Roman messenger of the gods), and while Uranus was in Virgo (an earth sign), many technological inventions were born (among them miniature solid-state circuitry and computers) that have revolutionized business, industry, and communications. Those born between 1964 and 1968 have Uranus conjunct Pluto in Virgo and are especially innovative and influential in these arenas. Overall, Uranus in Virgo confers ingenious and highly practical approaches to industry, science, technology, labor relations, and health care. They are revolutionary in these fields. This is the generation designated by the Zodiac and history to bear the burden of the hard work required to lay the practical foundations for the new Aquarian Age, ruled by Uranus, which is now upon us. They have an unusual talent for business and are diligent and resourceful workers. However, they are likely to experience many changes, disruptions, and upheavals in employment, as we have already seen with the "dot com" boom and bust and the collapse of the technology investment bubble. If Uranus is afflicted in Virgo, there can be erratic health problems. Given Virgo's concern with health, diet, and hygiene, under Uranus's influence this is the distinctly antismoking generation, with a strong interest in self-healing practices.

Uranus in Libra

This is a group of people with distinctly new ideas about marriage, partnerships, and the rules of social conduct. In marriage, the integrity of the relationship and individual freedom are far more important than any binding legal contract, which they regard as superfluous. Concerned with individual freedom, they are prone to experiment with open relationships, communal living, and new concepts of justice and morality and are likely to bring about reform and innovation of existing legal codes, especially those that govern marriage and partnerships. If Uranus is afflicted, there can be difficulties in marriage or partnerships due to carelessness or unreliability in handling mutual responsibilities.

Uranus in Scorpio

Uranus is the planet of revolutionary change, and Scorpio, the sign of death and renewal. Those born with Uranus in Scorpio are destined to see the destruction of the old order, out of the ashes of which the new order is born. Many who experienced

WWI were born with Uranus in Scorpio. Uranus was next in Scorpio between 1975 (the end of the Vietnam War) and 1982, a period that is believed to mark the beginning of the destruction of the Piscean Age from which the Aquarian Age will emerge, starting around 2000. Those born with Uranus in Scorpio have highly charged emotions and believe in taking swift and decisive action. They have no tolerance for any form of laziness, procrastination, or inactivity and tend to possess great scientific ingenuity. If Uranus is afflicted here, they can have violent tempers and be fiercely determined to bring about change at any cost, regardless of the havoc and destruction it might entail.

Uranus in Sagittarius

Uranus in Sagittarius is concerned with bringing about new concepts in religion, philosophy, and education. These natives will have an intense interest in foreign cultures and systems of belief and will travel widely and often. If Uranus is afflicted, there can be a dogmatic adherence to religious beliefs or a desire to negate all religious and spiritual thought. In the late 1890s and early 1900s, Uranus was in Sagittarius. It was a time of great intellectual ferment in the world of science, of Albert Einstein's first awakening, of the discovery of electro-magnetism, and of science going off into the realm of the invisible and the unknown—of the Sagittarian mental traveler, explorer, and pioneer. Sagittarius is interested not only in the idea but also in the "idea of the idea." Uranus's transit through the signs from Sagittarius to Pisces in the late 1890s to the early 1920s saw the great creative changes—artistic, scientific, social, and spiritual—that defined the twentieth century. From this Uranus entered Aries, the beginning of the new cycle or turn of the Great Wheel. With Uranus now transiting Pisces, we are once again at the end of a cycle, approaching a new era.

Uranus in Capricorn

These are people who will affect important changes within the power structures of both government and business, with a strong desire to change and improve the status quo in order to secure a prosperous future. They are concerned with bringing ideas into practical and concrete actuality. They seek constructive change, building the new on the foundations of the old, and therefore never fully do away with the past. They are ambitious, with a strong will to succeed, and are able to take old ideas and develop them in new ways, which they use to advance their careers. If Uranus is afflicted, they are likely to overextend themselves in the name of fulfilling their ambitions.

Uranus in Aquarius

Uranus rules Aquarius and is therefore powerfully placed when in this sign. Those with Uranus in Aquarius have an overall concern for the good of humanity. Their humanitarianism often extends to clairvoyance and a deep intuitive understanding of scientific as well as universal truths. They are open to new ideas and seek social reform through work with groups and organizations. Independent and strong-willed, they insist on making their own decisions and drawing their own conclusions. Objective and impartial, they will readily discard any ideas and methodologies that do not stand up to scientific scrutiny. Direct experience is, for them, the ultimate test of the validity of any matter. If Uranus is afflicted, license can be mistaken for freedom, and there can be unreasoning and willful stubbornness, eccentricity for its own sake, and an inability or refusal to work within any system requiring discipline or routine.

Uranus in Pisces

Uranus in Pisces confers strong intuitive abilities coupled with a keen scientific and psychological interest in the workings of the unconscious. Uranus was in Pisces during the 1920s, which saw the birth of Surrealism, along with the great artistic and literary movements of the twentieth century (see Neptune in Leo), and depth psychology. The great motivating drive for these individuals is to liberate the mind from the emotional influences and shackles of the past, to overcome the limitations of materialistic concerns, and to seek a higher spiritual understanding and identity. These individuals have strong religious inclinations that can border on the mystical. Many of their ideas and insights come to them through dreams. If Uranus is afflicted, there can be unrealistic idealism and an inability to cope with unpleasant situations; there can also be deception and untrustworthiness in dealings with others.

URANUS IN THE HOUSES

Uranus in the houses shows the type of activity through which we express the urge for individuality and freedom. It shows the circumstances in which sudden and exciting events enter our lives, the type of friends that we choose, and the kinds of activities that inspire us.

Uranus in the 1st House

Those with Uranus in the 1st House are driven by an irrepressible desire for personal freedom. They are restless and crave constant change and excitement, often preferring a life of risk and adventure to one of settlement and security. They have little regard for conventional behavior. A routine existence is anathema to them. Often they are seen as eccentric and exceptional individuals, and they tend to possess intuitive and unique talents in the arts or sciences. They are interested in the new and the inventive. These individuals are prone to extremes rather than moderation, and their behavior can be unpredictable. When Uranus is afflicted in the 1st House, eccentricity can become an end in and of itself; they can be unreasonably obstinate, and freedom can be pursued merely for its own sake, with little to no regard for consequences, responsibilities, or the rights of others. A well-aspected Uranus can produce individuals of real genius in their chosen fields.

Uranus in the 2nd House

Uranus in the 2nd House indicates unstable finances. These individuals are impulsive and reckless with their money and can spend it as fast as they make it. However, they can have an unusual talent for making money, especially through businesses involving inventions, electronics, and other scientific fields. If Uranus is afflicted, they can become involved in impractical financial ventures and experience trouble over unpaid debts.

Uranus in the 3rd House

Those with Uranus in the 3rd House are free thinkers with unusual and intuitive minds that are prone to sudden insights. Their thinking is not subject to the influence of others, and their ideas and opinions are based on direct experience and scientific fact. Impersonal and impartial, they are open to new ideas and always investigating the undiscovered and unusual. Many inventors and scientists have Uranus in the 3rd House. These people may also be involved in the communications media, especially radio and television. If Uranus is afflicted, the mind can be restless and scattered, prone to jumping hastily to conclusions and frequent changes of opinion.

Uranus in the 4th House

With Uranus in the 4th House, home and family life will be unusual, to say the least. Even the house itself may be of unusual or distinctive architecture and may contain any variety of electronic devices and gadgetry. Family members desire the freedom to come and go as they please, and there is the likelihood of one of the parents being exceptional or even strange in some regard. In this household, close friends are accepted as family members, and the home is a center for group activities. If Uranus is afflicted or in a mutable sign, there is the likelihood of sudden changes of residence and family and domestic situations. An afflicted Uranus can mean domestic upheavals and difficulties with family members. Relationships with parents and other family members are seldom binding.

Uranus in the 5th House

With Uranus in the 5th House there will be sudden and unusual romantic involvements that are prone to end as abruptly as they began. Romantic partners are themselves likely to be unusual or eccentric in some regard. Excitement here is sought through the pursuit of pleasure, and attitudes toward sexuality are often unconventional. An afflicted Uranus in the 5th House can mean excessive promiscuity. The children of these individuals are likely to be gifted in some regard, and their parents tend to give them a lot of freedom. If Uranus is afflicted, however, the children can suffer from psychological problems or abnormalities, and the parents may be neglectful of their responsibilities, especially in regard to proper discipline and the enforcement of the rules that children require and actually desire. Often, Uranus in the 5th House produces inspired and talented artists, especially in the electronics media. Many rock stars, movie actors, and television personalities have Uranus in the 5th House. An afflicted Uranus can instill antisocial behavior and a taste for unsavory forms of excitement. In marriage, an afflicted Uranus can mean extramarital affairs. In a woman's chart, there is a strong likelihood of pregnancy out of wedlock.

Uranus in the 6th House

Uranus in the 6th House indicates innovative and advanced methods employed in the name of both work and service. This can take the form of alternative approaches to healing, medicine, and diet, as well as working with advanced technology. Computer programmers and electronic engineers often have Uranus in the 6th House. Mathematical and scientific skills are indicative of Uranus in this house. Often, friends are made through work, as relationships with coworkers, employers, and employees are amicable and mentally stimulating. If Uranus is afflicted here, these relationships can be the exact opposite, riddled with conflict and strife. These people are highly sensitive to their working conditions and relationships and will leave a job if these are unsatisfactory. They require freedom to do their work in their own way and will rebel against strict or rigid supervision. Uranus in the 6th House can indicate involvement with labor unions. If Uranus is afflicted, employment can be unstable, changing often and ending suddenly. Ill health can result from excessive nervousness.

Uranus in the 7th House

With Uranus in the 7th House, there is a strong desire for freedom in marriage and other personal relationships. If Uranus is afflicted, divorce is likely, as the need for independence will be far stronger than any sense of commitment to the marriage. Marriage is often sudden and under unusual circumstances, and the spouse is often eccentric or brilliant in some regard. Other relationships tend to be either very close or superficial, shallow, and fleeting. Mercurial changes of mood, attitudes, and opinions can leave others angry and confused.

Uranus in the 8th House

Uranus in the 8th House denotes a quest for freedom of expression through esoteric traditions and/or sexuality. As the 8th House involves other people's resources, the individual may receive an unexpected inheritance or benefit from his or her business or marriage partners. Uranus in the 8th can also indicate an intense and unusual dream life, and people with this placement are often very intuitive.

Uranus in the 9th House

Uranus in the 9th House confers highly evolved, advanced, and innovative ideas in regard to philosophy, religion, and higher education. Ideas about education will be especially progressive, with interest in new methods of teaching. Religious views are often unorthodox, with an interest in the occult and the esoteric. These individuals are likely to travel far and wide in search of new experiences and ideas. They have a keen interest in the remote past and the distant future. An afflicted Uranus here can mean a fanatical adherence to superstitious cults and political dogmas.

Uranus in the 10th House

Uranus in the 10th House often indicates an unusual profession and an outstanding or unique reputation within its ranks. These individuals are apt to be leaders and innovators in their chosen fields. They are generally politically liberal or radical, almost certainly never conservative. These people have a driving ambition to achieve prominence and make unique contributions in their professions. However, changes in fortune can be sudden and drastic. An afflicted Uranus can be evident in political extremism and revolutionary tendencies and may also indicate a sudden rise followed by an equally sudden fall.

Uranus in the 11th House

Those with Uranus in the 11th House, which corresponds to Aquarius, are open-minded, impartial, and humanitarian in their outlook. They have little to no regard for traditional opinions and mores in the face of objective truth, which they have an intuitive ability to perceive, along with universal laws and principles. Often, they have many unusual friendships and group associations that are mentally and spiritually stimulating. They have an impersonal attitude to marriage and romantic partnerships, possessing a bohemian desire for freedom. Their desire for new stimulation often makes them unwilling to be limited by a single relationship, and they are tolerant of similar attitudes and behavior in others. If Uranus is afflicted, friendships can be unstable and even treacherous. These individuals can be unreliable and inconsiderate regarding commitments to friends and other associations. Their selfish motivations and behavior are more than likely to elicit a negative backlash as a result of lovers and friends feeling that they are being used, disregarded, or treated in a disrespectful or offhanded manner.

Uranus in the 12th House

Uranus in the 12th House indicates the mystical quest for spiritual identity and a deep probing into the hidden recesses of the unconscious. Interest in and understanding of esoteric teachings and practices such as yoga and meditation are likely. Intuitive and psychic abilities may be highly developed. If Uranus is afflicted, the individual can suffer from delusions and a general confusion caused by neurosis and dabbling in negative psychic practices and phenomena.

ASPECTS OF URANUS

Aspects of Uranus, as well as the sign and house position, are indicators of our originality and inventiveness. The affairs ruled by the planets aspected by Uranus are subject to sudden and dramatic changes, as a result of the planet's influence. These can be positive or negative, depending on the aspects. If Uranus is afflicted, we may be prone toward erratic, unreliable, and reckless behavior or have eccentric attitudes toward the areas of life under Uranus's influence. The true freedom offered by Uranus can only be acquired after we have learned Saturn's lesson—that lasting, life-affirming freedom is earned only when it is based on self-discipline.

Uranus Conjunctions

Uranus conjunctions are indicative of individuals who are original, willful, creative, and capable of dynamic action. Humanitarian and friendly, they are never bound by tradition and are fiercely independent. Their lives are marked by sudden changes. These attributes will be most evident in the affairs ruled by the planet or planets forming the conjunction, and the signs and houses Uranus and the planet(s) occupy and rule.

Uranus Sextiles

Uranus sextiles mean that the individual will encounter sudden opportunities for mental growth and expansion as a result of his or her openness and enthusiasm for new ideas. These people are clever, intuitive, and often scientifically inclined. They communicate well, make friends easily, and are attracted to groups and organizations. Their abilities will be manifested most strongly in the affairs ruled by the planet or planets forming the sextile and the signs and houses Uranus and the planet(s) rule and occupy.

Uranus Squares

Uranus squares indicate individuals who are likely to thwart their own success through instability and impulsive actions. They tend to be fickle, willful, unreasonable and obstinate, refusing to heed the good advice of others and stumbling blindly into catastrophe. These tendencies will be most notable in the affairs ruled by the planet or planets that form the square and the signs and houses that Uranus and the planet(s) rule and occupy.

Uranus Trines

Trines of Uranus indicate sudden and unexpected good fortune. These individuals are intuitive, creative, and original in the way they go about doing things and will have many friends and interesting and unusual adventures. The benefits of this configuration will be most evident in the affairs ruled by the planet or planets forming the trine and in the signs and houses that Uranus and the planet(s) rule and occupy.

Uranus Oppositions

Uranus oppositions denote problems with relationships resulting from a demanding, unreasonable, and unpredictable attitude toward others. These individuals tend to be willfully erratic, unreliable, and selfishly obsessed with their own personal desires. This will be most evident in the affairs ruled by the planet or planets that oppose Uranus and in the signs and houses that Uranus and those planet(s) rule and occupy.

CHAPTER 13

NEPTUNE

Neptune is the planet of mysticism. Its power of dissolution can blur personal boundaries, making us aware of our interconnectedness, capable of artistic accomplishment that speaks to many people, and reaching the heights of spiritual attainment. Yet the same dissolving power can lead us into delusion if our self-awareness and ego, represented by the Sun, are weak.

NEPTUNE IN THE SIGNS

The next in the transpersonal planets after Uranus, Neptune spends about thirteen years in each sign. Thus, the sign position of Neptune has more generational significance than it does personal.

Neptune in Aries (1861/62–1874/75)

Neptune in Aries indicates a strong concern with mystical and religious concepts. The initiative and drive for spiritual creativity and regeneration mean that pioneering advances are made in these fields, and it is interesting to note the popularity of spiritualism, the occult, Eastern religions, and the like among this generation in the late nineteenth and early twentieth centuries. Spiritual pride and egotism, and the use of this knowledge for personal power and self-aggrandizement, are the dark side of this expression.

Neptune in Taurus (1874/75–1887/89)

Here, there is a strong idealism regarding the proper use of money and resources, with an active seeking of practical applications for idealistic visions and theories. On the negative side, there can be a preoccupation with money and materialism.

Neptune in Gemini (1887/89–1901/02)

This is the generation that produced the likes of Ernest Hemingway, William Faulkner, F. Scott Fitzgerald, John Steinbeck, and Aldous Huxley—those who have much to do with giving creative expression to the intuitive and image-making faculties of the mind through poetry and literature. These people are gifted with highly active and versatile imaginations and are able to channel and communicate ideas from the collective consciousness. When negative, there may be a superficial preoccupation with the dream world and confusion in thinking and communication.

Neptune in Cancer (1901/2–1914/16)

This is a generation with strong psychic ties to home (including their native country), family, and the earth. They are emotionally sensitive and sympathetic and, if Neptune is strongly placed (on the cusp of the 4th House or in the 12th) and aspected, can have psychic and mediumistic tendencies. When negative, there can be maudlin sentimentality and an exclusive attachment to family and country.

Neptune in Leo (1914/16–1928/29)

This is a generation with strong musical and artistic talents, with a special interest in the theater and other performing arts. Neptune in Leo is also strongly inclined to romantic idealism in love and courtship. On the negative side, this romanticism can lead to self-delusion in matters of the heart, along with extravagant spending in pursuit of pleasure and impracticality in dealing with children. Neptune was in Leo during the Roaring Twenties, that period of opulent extravagance, wild carousing, and reckless stock speculation which led directly to the stock market crash of 1929 and the Great Depression. As F. Scott Fitzgerald wrote at the time, "I have lost my glittering mirage." Neptune is the planet of illusions. The movie industry is also included under its rulership. Uranus was in Pisces during this same period, in which the movie industry was born along with the seminal artistic and literary movements of the twentieth century. Also notable during this time was the publication of C. G. Jung's original insights into the unconscious and the process of individuation (Jung himself was a Leo).

Neptune in Virgo (1928/29–1942/43)

Neptune is in its detriment in Virgo, the opposite sign of Pisces, of which Neptune is one of the rulers. This is a generation whose creative and imaginative faculties and endeavors are blocked by adverse material circumstances. Neptune was in Virgo through the Great Depression, a time of mass unemployment and poverty. Employment is ruled by Virgo. Neptune in Virgo can also cause psychosomatic illnesses and doubt and negativity toward intuitive and emotional responses. There can be an overconcern, perhaps as a result of insecurity and deprivation, with materialistic values, as well as an excessive preoccupation with unimportant details. Unhealthy dietary practices are also another manifestation of Neptune in Virgo, and it was during this time that much of the chemical adulteration of our food supply began.

Neptune in Libra (1942/43–1955/57)

Neptune in Libra has a natural instinct for emotional and social conformity. On the negative side, this can mean a blind adherence to social movements and trends. However, there is also a strong intuitive awareness of social relationships and responsibilities. Mutual social responsibility is based more on the spirit than the letter of the law. Neptune in Libra can give rise to new forms of art.

Neptune in Scorpio (1955/57–1970)

Scorpio is the sex sign, and Neptune rules drugs. Neptune in Scorpio is a period in which the natural desires are exploited. There is much emotional intensity and confusion, causing the turmoil within the unconscious to break out. This period was marked by the exploitation of sex for commercial purposes. Many were tainted as a result, while a few managed to experience a spiritual epiphany leading to a search into life's inner mysteries. Sexual permissiveness and promiscuity led to the widespread outbreak of venereal diseases, along with drug use as a means of psychological escape.

Neptune in Sagittarius (1970–1984)

Neptune in Sagittarius signifies a period of higher spiritual and religious values and an intuitive exploration of the mysteries of the mind. There is much foreign travel and exchange of ideas, and artistic expression is also spiritually oriented. The negative manifestations of this period tend to be aimless wandering, both physically and mentally, and fanatical adherence to wrong-minded religious cults, false prophets, and charlatan gurus.

Neptune in Capricorn (1984–2000)

This is a period in which world governments are in chaos, and economic and political structures are in upheaval. In our time, it is the karmic summation of the Piscean Age, out of which many reach new heights of spiritual enlightenment and the new Aquarian Age is born. Spiritual responsibility for the world is here expressed in practical ways. Some astrologers believe that this period has already heralded the beginnings of world government.

Neptune in Aquarius (2000–2013)

Neptune entered Aquarius along with Uranus in 2000, marking the true beginning of the Aquarian Age. It is supposed to see the birth of a new civilization based on humanitarianism, globalization, science, and technology.

Neptune in Pisces (2013–2026)

This will be a time of peace following the upheavals of the birth of the Aquarian Age. The highest form of Aquarian culture will begin, making use of the greatest accomplishments of the Piscean Age, expressing itself in exalted forms of music and art. Great strides will be made in medicine and healing. During this period many great artists, mystics, teachers, and spiritual leaders will be born.

NEPTUNE IN THE HOUSES

Neptune in the houses indicates how we use our image-making faculties or ability to visualize. It points to those circumstances in life that are affected by dreams, premonitions, and deep intuitive insights. It also indicates the meaning and nature of the karma produced by our past actions. When Neptune is afflicted, its house position shows those areas in life in which we may be prone to self-delusion and being unrealistic.

Neptune in the 1st House

Those with Neptune in the 1st House, the house of the *I am*, have a strong, sensitive, and intuitive awareness of self and environment. A strongly aspected Neptune can confer clairvoyant abilities and a deep understanding of the motives underlying human actions and events. When positively aspected, inspired mystical visions are a distinct possibility, as well as significant artistic and musical talents. If Neptune is afflicted here, there is the danger of being susceptible to negative psychic influences and forces, and the use of drugs and alcohol should be assiduously avoided. An afflicted Neptune here can cause unreliability, self-delusion, alcoholism, drug addiction, and a loose and aimless lifestyle.

Neptune in the 2nd House

Those with Neptune in the 2nd House are idealistic about the use of money and material resources. They are prone to donate generously to humanitarian causes and be liberal with their material resources. If Neptune is well aspected, the individual will have an intuitive ability to make money and acquire wealth. These individuals tend be extravagant, and money may come and go through mysterious or unusual circumstances. If Neptune is afflicted here, they can find themselves frequently in a financial muddle. They may be impractical, lazy about, or slow to choose their means of earning a living, relying on others for financial support.

Neptune in the 3rd House

Those with Neptune in the 3rd House have a great capacity for mental visualization, especially if Neptune aspects Mercury. Telepathic abilities are often an attribute of Neptune in the 3rd House, making them channels of information that they are compelled to share impartially with others. If Neptune is well aspected, intuition can be put to practical use, especially if Neptune is in an earth sign. An afflicted Neptune may indicate learning difficulties, absentmindedness, and a tendency to become lost in fantasy and daydreaming. There may be misunderstandings or conflicts with siblings and neighbors and confusion in communication, especially when traveling. Great care should be exercised in making contracts and agreements.

Neptune in the 4th House

With Neptune in the 4th House, there will be strong unconscious emotional ties to home and family that are karmic in nature. People with Neptune in the 4th House often live near water and have strong feelings for the land and nature. Family secrets and mysteries surrounding aspects of home life are common. These people have a deep desire to mother the world and often bring strays and strangers into their homes. An afflicted Neptune can cause confused family relationships and a chaotic domestic environment. Neurosis from difficulties with parents and other family members can arise, and emotionally based nervous disorders that are difficult to diagnose may develop later in life.

Neptune in the 5th House

Those with Neptune in the 5th House have a strong unconscious desire for love and appreciation through romance and creative self-expression. They are naturally gifted performers, with a general love of the theater. Unusual circumstances often surround romantic and sexual involvements. An afflicted Neptune can indicate secret love affairs and sexual entanglements. Disappointments in love are likely. A well-aspected Neptune often means intuitive insight into the workings of the stock market, although these people need to be cautious with investments and speculations. Their children will be highly sensitive and intuitive individuals. If Neptune is afflicted, however, their children may suffer from psychological problems and be hard to cope with. Children may also be adopted or born out of wedlock. An afflicted Neptune can also indicate a broken family from which the children suffer.

Neptune in the 6th House

Neptune in the 6th House puts spiritual emphasis on work and service. Neptune is in its detriment in the 6th House, meaning that many sacrifices will be demanded and the lessons of work and health will be difficult to learn. A well-aspected Neptune, however, can provide an intuitive understanding of how to work efficiently and effectively. These individuals may well be interested in alternative medicine (especially homeopathy and other vibrational therapies), diet, and spiritual healing. There is a strong inclination to care for animals and even communicate with them telepathically. An afflicted Neptune can subject the individual to psychosomatic illnesses and infections that are hard to cure, as well as hypochondria and mental illness. Also, unemployment and unsatisfactory working conditions and relationships are likely. If Neptune is well aspected, working conditions will be harmonious, and there will be close emotional bonds with coworkers, employees, and employers. Work may be related to psychotherapy. These individuals often work in hospitals, schools, and other large institutions.

Neptune in the 7th House

Neptune in the 7th House indicates that there are strong karmic connections in marriage and partnerships. There may even be a tight psychic link with the spouse and an intuitive understanding of people in general. Those with Neptune in the 7th House are highly sensitive to the moods and feelings of those around them. When Neptune is well aspected, spiritual values are applied to relations with others, manifested as compassion and understanding. The achievement of an ideal spiritual marriage is a distinct possibility. If Neptune is afflicted, emotional confusion can cause difficulties in marriage, and individuals can be easily deceived and misled by others. They can also be vague or unreliable concerning partnerships and social responsibilities. When badly afflicted, these people can themselves be deliberately deceptive or psychologically twisted, and there is a strong possibility of lawsuits and public scandal.

Neptune in the 8th House

Neptune in the 8th House indicates powerful psychic tendencies, often with an interest in the occult and spiritualism or communication with the dead. Secretive or deceptive circumstances may surround a partner's money and financial assets. A well-aspected Neptune can confer clairvoyant abilities. An afflicted 8th-House Neptune can indicate mysterious and bizarre losses and difficulties with a partner's finances, often caused by deception either by the individual or some other party or parties involved. This can be particularly true in financial matters surrounding death.

Neptune in the 9th House

Neptune in the 9th House shows a keen interest in mysticism and religion. This is a highly impressionable mind, capable of intuitive insights and prophetic visions. An afflicted 9th-House Neptune can mean fanatical adherence to dubious cults and spiritual leaders. The individual may also be impractical about obtaining a proper education, neglecting to finish or get the necessary training required for a job; marriage will bring problems with relatives.

Neptune in the 10th House

Here, intuition will play an important part in the individual's career. It is considered an excellent position for psychiatrists, psychologists, and ministers. One of the parents is likely to be unusual in some way, and the 10th-House Neptune individual's work will be unusual and surrounded by strange circumstances. Many actors, artists, and musicians have Neptune in the 10th House. A well-aspected Neptune can bring honor as a result of outstanding personal achievement or sacrifice. An afflicted Neptune can indicate professional ineptitude and impracticality, often resulting in an inability to get along with employers. Scandal or loss of reputation may also result from dishonesty or irresponsibility on the job.

Neptune in the 11th House

With Neptune in the 11th House, there will be idealistic and unusual friendships and group associations, with whom the individual forms close spiritual links. These individuals are generous with friends, from whom they in turn receive spiritual guidance and assistance in the realization of their goals. They are sensitive to the needs of humanity and may join philanthropic or spiritual groups and organizations. If Neptune is afflicted, friendships can be unreliable and so-called friends can even become secret enemies. Unwholesome associations can lead to self-undoing, and there is a danger of alcoholism and drug abuse. These people must learn to be discriminating in their choice of friends and associates. An afflicted Neptune can also mean an impractical and misguided idealism.

Neptune in the 12th House

Here, Neptune confers a strong intuitive link to the deep unconscious, often resulting in mystical religious tendencies. These individuals will tend to seek seclusion and privacy in order to expedite the inner spiritual search. They have a sense of memories from previous incarnations and gain much spiritual wisdom from this intuitive link to the past. A well-aspected Neptune confers clairvoyant and healing abilities, along with literary, artistic, and musical talents. An afflicted Neptune may result in a dark and neurotic preoccupation with the problems of the past, creating mental and emotional confusion and a subjective withdrawal from the affairs of daily practical life. An afflicted Neptune in Pisces can make these people extremely vulnerable to deeply rooted unconscious fears and neurosis.

ASPECTS OF NEPTUNE

Aspects of Neptune, along with the house and sign position, indicate those areas in our life that can be directly affected by psychic or transcendental influences. When well aspected, this often expresses itself through art and music. Neptune rules the film industry, an art and industry of visual illusions, and this expression also takes the form of drama, photography, and cinematography. Suffice it to say that spiritual inspiration manifests itself through a talent for imagery. Often, people with Neptune aspects are capable of sending and receiving visual images telepathically. If Neptune is afflicted, self-deception and unrealistic goals and desires will plague the individual in regard to the affairs ruled by the planets afflicting it, along with the signs and houses that Neptune and the planet(s) occupy and rule.

Neptune Conjunctions

Conjunctions of Neptune indicate great depth of emotional and spiritual comprehension and compassion. Often, these individuals have strong psychic abilities, and their mystical tendencies and attitudes can make them seem otherworldly and their actions at times difficult to comprehend, although, in the end, those very same actions end up making a strange kind of sense beyond the veil of the mundane world. If the conjunction is afflicted, the individuals can suffer from delusions and tend to ignore reality. These characteristics will be manifested in the affairs ruled by the planet or planets conjuncting Neptune, and the signs and houses occupied and ruled by Neptune and the conjuncting planet(s).

Neptune Sextiles

Neptune sextiles indicate opportunities for mental and spiritual growth through the creative use of the imagination. This may be expressed through writing, communication, friendships, and group associations that embrace idealistic causes. These proclivities will be most evident in the affairs ruled by the planet or planets forming the sextile and the signs and houses that Neptune and the planet(s) rule and occupy.

Neptune Squares

Squares of Neptune are indicative of confusion and destructive tendencies that are the product of neuroses and negative conditioning. There is a strong inclination to avoid responsibility and facing reality, sometimes manifesting itself as alcohol and drug abuse. These tendencies will be most evident in the affairs ruled by the planet or planets that form the square with Neptune, and the signs and houses Neptune and the planet(s) rule and occupy.

Neptune Trines

Neptune trines indicate good fortune and gain through the creative use of the imagination, as well as a capacity for deep spiritual insight. These characteristics will be manifested most strongly in the affairs ruled by the planet or planets that trine Neptune and the signs and houses Neptune and the planet(s) occupy and rule.

Neptune Oppositions

Neptune oppositions indicate that there will be relationship problems resulting from the individual being deceptive and unreliable, tendencies that stem from deep psychological problems. These individuals often believe their own lies and tend to project their psychological problems onto others. The result is misunderstanding and confusion, as others never know where they stand or what the truth is. This will be most evident in the affairs ruled by the planet or planets that oppose Neptune and the signs and houses Neptune and the planet(s) occupy and rule.

CHAPTER 14

PLUTO

Pluto's orbit is so elusive and erratic that although astronomers were noticing its effects upon Uranus (discovered in 1781) and Neptune (discovered in 1846), it wasn't pinpointed until 1930. Its secretive nature makes it an apt ruler for Scorpio. Pluto, the Lord of the Underworld, rules death and transformation and the wielding of power.

PLUTO IN THE SIGNS

Pluto is the slowest moving of the planets, taking approximately 248 years to make a complete transit through the Zodiac. Due to its eccentric orbit, the number of years it spends in each sign varies from twelve to thirty-two. Along with Uranus and Neptune, its sign position is more historical and generational than personal.

Pluto in Aries (1823–1852)

Aries is the sign of individual will and new experience, the beginning of a new cycle of action. Pluto in Aries saw the American expansion into the West and the golden age of the pioneer, a period of both dauntless courage in the name of freedom and settling a new frontier and ruthless violence and bloodshed in the struggle for land and riches. In Europe and Asia, revolutionary movements (the revolutions of 1848 in Europe, the Taiping Rebellion in China) heralded the beginning of the overthrow of the ancient order in the name of the new.

Pluto in Taurus (1852–1884)

Taurus is the sign of material resources and monetary concerns, and Pluto in Taurus marked a period of great economic expansion in which the Industrial Revolution reached its peak and corporations came into being.

Pluto in Gemini (1884–1914)

Gemini rules ideas, communication, and inventiveness, and Pluto in Gemini was a period of great scientific discoveries and important inventions. The discovery and harnessing of electricity set the stage for the development of modern technology and communications. The telephone, automobile, and airplane are among the many significant inventions of this period.

Pluto in Cancer (1914–1939)

Cancer is the sign of the Mother, the home, land, environment, food production, and personal and instinctive emotional expression. Pluto in Cancer was a time of economic struggle and the growth of strong nationalist sentiment that led finally to the outbreak of WWII. It also saw a revolution in agriculture with the building of dams and the introduction of pesticides and chemical fertilizers. The threats to family and national security gave birth to new political philosophies—the New Deal in the United States, fascism in Europe and Japan, and communism in Russia and China.

Pluto in Leo (1939–1957)

Leo is the sign of expressive will, power, and leadership. Pluto in Leo saw the outbreak of WWII and a renewed thrust for world domination, the development of atomic energy (ruled by Pluto), and the unleashing of the atomic bomb. Humanity faced the possibility of the total destruction of civilization alongside the heights of technological achievement and the harnessing of awesome power. The end of WWII gave birth to many new sovereign nations from the ashes of the old colonial empires and the global power struggle between capitalism and communism.

Pluto in Virgo (1957–1972)

Virgo is the sign of work, service, health, and the practical application of technology. Pluto in Virgo marked a period of revolutionary changes in industry, employment, and medicine. Computers revolutionized science, business, and industry; automation replaced many workers; and great strides and discoveries were made in medicine and science. America landed the first man on the Moon. The development of prepackaged food and the chemical adulteration and pollution of the food supply led to the widespread advocacy and promotion of organic food in the 1960s, while at the same time psychedelic drugs opened up formerly unknown realms of consciousness that brought about massive social upheavals. Pluto rules Scorpio, the sign of sexuality and reproductive health, and this period saw the development of birth control and a new sexual morality.

Pluto in Libra (1972–1984)

Libra is the sign of justice, human relations, social expression, and psychology. Pluto in Libra saw the awakening of a new consciousness of social responsibility and the development of new concepts of marriage, law, and justice. Civil rights laws were strengthened, divorce was made easier, and America's involvement in Vietnam ended during this period, largely due to the growing antiwar movement both at home and abroad.

Pluto in Scorpio (1984–2000)

Pluto has its fastest orbital motion while passing through Libra and Scorpio. Pluto rules Scorpio, the sign of death and rebirth. This is by far the most potent of all the planetary sign positions, marking the end of the Piscean Age and a period in which the consequences of human action or inaction will be felt profoundly on a grand scale. According to astrological lore, this is a period in which the danger of plague, famine, and biological and atomic warfare are at their highest. Humanity is forced by necessity to change and regenerate in preparation for the Age of Aquarius, which began in 2000.

Pluto in Sagittarius (2000-?)

Sagittarius is the sign of religion, law, philosophy and education, of ideas ruling action. Pluto in Sagittarius marks the
beginning of a new age of enlightenment and spiritual regeneration. New spiritual leaders will arise to teach the fundamental laws governing life and the universe, and new
scientific discoveries and theories will result in a more comprehensive understanding of the underlying forces behind all
existence. A recent example of this is String Theory, which,
interestingly enough, harkens back to the theories of
Pythagoras.

Pluto in Capricorn (1762-1777)

Capricorn is the sign dealing with political and economic
power structures, ambition, status, and leadership. Pluto in
Capricorn saw the birth of new concepts of government, the
most notable of which was the American Declaration of
Independence in 1776. This period saw the birth of democratic governments and the displacement of aristocratic
power structures. Pluto in Capricorn manifests itself as a
dynamic and practical will in organization, business, and government, based on the concept that all human beings are enti-
tled to a fair chance to develop their own potential according
to their abilities—the right to "life, liberty, and the pursuit of
happiness."

Pluto in Aquarius (1777-1799)

Aquarius is the sign of group associations and activities, science, and humanitarianism. Pluto in Aquarius witnessed the

American War of Independence and the drafting of the United States Constitution and the Bill of Rights. This period also marked the French Revolution, a major revolt of the common masses (ruled by Aquarius) against an archaic and corrupt form of government, and the first major European social experiment in political freedom. The next transit of Pluto through Aquarius will be a period of major scientific discovery and global unity.

Pluto in Pisces (1799–1823)

Pisces is the sign of the deep unconscious, mystical experience, and intuitive, creative artistic expression. Pluto in Pisces was a period of great cultural change and innovation that saw the creation of many great works of art of lasting meaning and value.

PLUTO IN THE HOUSES

Pluto in the houses shows those areas in life in which we must exercise conscious, creative willpower over our self and environment. Pluto deals with issues of mass destiny, and its house position shows the individual effects and personal interpretations of these changes and how mass or collective karma is linked to individual karma.

Pluto in the 1st House

This position indicates an individual with an intense spiritual self-awareness and strong willpower. His or her childhood is often marked by extreme hardship, acquainting the individual with life's struggle for survival at an early age, an experience that makes for a guarded loner who hides his or her innermost feelings. Such a person can seem aloof and difficult to get to know. In physical appearance, 1st-House Pluto people can have a robust build and intensely penetrating eyes. They possess considerable initiative but find it difficult to cooperate with others or conform to traditional conduct and mores. Pluto is accidentally dignified in the 1st House, for it is one of the rulers of Aries, the "natural resident" of the 1st House. Thus, Pluto here confers a highly developed sense of personal power and will. The strong individualism and innate nonconformity of this position can make it difficult for the individual to get along at home, in marriage, and in professional relationships. If Pluto is in conjunction with the Ascendant and strongly aspected, the individual may possess clairvoyant abilities.

Pluto in the 2nd House

Pluto in the 2nd House confers a driving ambition to obtain money and material resources. As Pluto rules Scorpio and the 8th House, which is opposite Taurus and the 2nd House, this can indicate that these ambitions are likely to be met through the use of other people's money. A well-aspected Pluto here connotes great resourcefulness in money-making through the ability to perceive hidden financial possibilities. An afflicted Pluto in the 2nd House can indicate greediness and selfishness; as a result, friends can be lost and there can be trouble with lawsuits and taxes. The great lesson of Pluto in the 2nd House is that material resources are fluid and must be used for the benefit of all.

Pluto in the 3rd House

Pluto in the 3rd House bestows mental resourcefulness and scientific abilities upon the individual, with an innate and penetrating comprehension of the causes underlying life's experiences and manifestations. Generally, these individuals have strong opinions and will only compromise their beliefs in the face of factual evidence to the contrary. Often, they are privy to secret or exclusive information pertaining to matters of great importance, and what they think and communicate can have serious consequences. They are also likely to travel in secret and for mysterious reasons and have strange encounters and experiences. If Pluto is afflicted, scheming and plotting can cause trouble with siblings, neighbors, and coworkers.

Pluto in the 4th House

Here, the individual is inclined to be master of the home and family. If Pluto is afflicted, a dominating attitude is likely to alienate family members. If Pluto is well aspected, the person can be very resourceful in providing for and improving the domestic situation, as well as possessing a powerful psychic connection to the earth that bestows an intuitive knowledge of its mysteries and hidden resources. An afflicted Pluto here can mean the death of one of the parents at an early age. There may be mysterious or strange circumstances in regard to home and family. There is also the danger of a power struggle with other members of the family or household residents.

Pluto in the 5th House

Pluto in the 5th House is an indicator of creative power that can find its expression in many forms—through art, love, procreation, and nurturing. A well-aspected Pluto here can inspire profound works of art. Spiritual regeneration is experienced through love, and the individual's offspring can be blessed with talent, genius, and self-determination. If Pluto is afflicted here, there is the danger of self-degradation through sexual excess. The individual may dominate or be dominated by the romantic partner and take a severe attitude toward his or her children. Serious losses can be incurred through speculation.

Pluto in the 6th House

Pluto in the 6th House confers an ability to improve existing work methods and employment, and conscientious hard work toward this aim will bring financial gain and recognition. These people also apply their will to improve their health by adopting correct dietary practices, exercise, and mental discipline. People involved in construction, salvage, and atomic energy programs often have Pluto in the 6th House. A badly afflicted Pluto here can mean that serious attention must be paid to personal health. There can be a tendency to be overbearing and uncooperative with coworkers, employees, and employers, thus jeopardizing job security, and dishonesty at work could cause legal problems.

Pluto in the 7th House

With Pluto in the 7th House, the individual's life will experience drastic alteration as a result of marriage and other partnerships, both personal and professional. The individual tends to attract a partner who is strong-willed and domineering. Here, Pluto imbues a strong sense of justice that reacts intensely against the wrongdoings of others. If Pluto is well aspected, there can be a profound intuitive insight into other people and their motives. Pluto being accidentally in its detriment in the 7th House indicates a tendency to dominate or to be dominated by others. It is important for those with Pluto in this position to strive for a balanced sharing of initiative and responsibility in their relationships and dealings with others.

Pluto in the 8th House

Pluto in the 8th House confers a fierce and powerful will along with strong psychic and clairvoyant abilities. These people have an innate and deep understanding of the transmigration of the soul, karma, and other issues of life after physical death. This intuitive awareness of the invisible behind the visible can give a profound insight into subjects that deal with the nature of energy and matter, such as physics. The individual is also often able to rejuvenate the discarded resources of others. Life is taken very seriously, with no time for trivialities and often a severe do-or-die attitude. When Pluto is well aspected, the individual will show great strength and resourcefulness in times of crisis. Many activities will be carried out secretively, revealing themselves only in their final stages. An afflicted Pluto can mean serious problems with a partner's finances and the use of underhanded methods, including manipulative psychic powers, to gain control of the resources of others.

Pluto in the 9th House

Pluto in the 9th House indicates a strong interest in improving legal, educational, moral, and philosophical systems.

There is an intuitive ability to identify fundamental problems within the larger social order, bestowing a profound insight into the future of humanity. A strongly aspected Pluto here can mean the individual has a capacity for spiritual leadership. They can experience great achievements through higher education and have little tolerance for hypocrisy or injustice. Yet, ambition to achieve distinction, when carried too far, can result in excessive pride and competitiveness. An afflicted Pluto can produce a religious fanatic determined to impose his or her beliefs upon others.

Pluto in the 10th House

Pluto in the 10th House, the house ruled by Capricorn, indicates a strong will and a relentless drive to succeed. There is an equally compelling desire to reform and rehabilitate existing power structures, which can make for powerful friends as well as enemies. These individuals are often misunderstood and controversial figures. Crises in their careers may well force them to change their professions. They can be leaders in science as well as politics. Adept at handling positions of power, this is a favorable position for politicians and other work in public institutions. When Pluto is well aspected, farsightedness can lead to wise leadership. An afflicted Pluto can cause dictatorial tendencies, alienation from others, and a blind ambition driven by purely selfish motives.

Pluto in the 11th House

Here, reformist tendencies are expressed through friendships and group associations, and these individuals possess an immense capacity for dynamic group leadership through which scientific and humanitarian advances are achieved. Pluto is accidentally in its detriment in the 11th House, and the individual must be very careful about respecting the rights of others and to use his or her will cooperatively in order to work effectively within the group. Selfish or egotistical motivations will lead to financial losses, disappointments in love, and trouble over joint resources and taxes. Health, employment, friendships, and home life can all suffer. A well-aspected Pluto can confer a penetrating intuitive insight and scientific genius.

Pluto in the 12th House

Those with Pluto in the 12th House have profound insight and clairvoyant abilities. The need here is to regenerate the unconscious mind by bringing its contents into consciousness. A well-aspected Pluto here confers a deep sympathy and ability to assist and improve the conditions of the less fortunate, along with an intuitive understanding of life's so-called occult mysteries. These individuals are telepathically sensitive to the thoughts, feelings, and motives of others. This may cause them to withdraw into privacy or seclusion, and to even take covert action against those who have crossed them in some way. Mental preoccupation with their own problems can lead to an inability to get along with others at work. An afflicted Pluto can also indicate secret enemies capable of considerable treachery or neurotic problems and a danger of involvement with destructive psychic forces.

ASPECTS OF PLUTO

Aspects of Pluto, as well as its house and sign position, show those areas in life where we are able to renew or revitalize our expression of personal will. Pluto represents a principle of fundamental will or energy that is capable of completely altering the quality of our life. This power can be used for good or evil, to regenerate or degrade the affairs ruled by the planets that Pluto aspects, along with the signs and houses that Pluto and the planet(s) occupy and rule. Pluto also indicates how our lives are altered by forces beyond our personal control.

Pluto Conjunctions

Pluto conjunctions indicate the power to transform one's nature and mode of expression. This can be for better or for worse. These individuals have strong wills, penetrating insight, and great powers of concentration. There is a likelihood of possessing an interest in science, especially nuclear physics. These qualities will be most apparent in the affairs ruled by the planet or planets forming the conjunction, and the signs and houses Pluto and the planet(s) rule and occupy.

Pluto Sextiles

Pluto sextiles indicate opportunities for self-transformation and mental growth through the dynamic exercise of personal willpower. These individuals tend to leave their mark upon the world through writing, communication, and their association with group endeavors. This will be most apparent in the affairs ruled by the planet or planets that form the sextile and in the signs and houses Pluto and the planet(s) rule and occupy.

Pluto Squares

Pluto squares are indicative of individuals who create difficulties for themselves that are the direct result of their own ruthless desires. Often they attempt the impossible, and their overbearing impatience and dictatorial attitude ultimately defeat their purpose. These tendencies will be most apparent in the affairs ruled by the planet or planets that form the square and in the signs and houses Pluto and the planet(s) rule and occupy.

Pluto Trines

Pluto trines mean that good fortune and spiritual development will result from the creative use of willpower and mental concentration to bring about transformation of oneself and one's environment. Many clairvoyants, healers, and spiritual teachers have this aspect in their horoscope. These effects will be felt most strongly in those areas ruled by the planet or planets forming the trine and the signs and houses Pluto and the planet(s) occupy and rule.

Pluto Oppositions

Pluto oppositions point to problems with relationships stemming from demanding, dictatorial, and domineering attitudes. These individuals wish to reform and control others without any consideration or respect for their rights and desires. As a result, they often find themselves resented and ostracized. These effects will be most strongly felt in relationships involving the affairs ruled by the planet or planets opposing Pluto and in the signs and houses Pluto and the planet(s) rule and occupy.

ABOUT THE AUTHOR

DAMIAN SHARP was born in Australia and is the recipient of two Literary Fellowship Awards from the Australian Council for the Arts. He is the author of *Simple Feng Shui* and *Simple Chinese Astrology* and has published short stories in periodicals such as the *Chicago Review*. He lives in San Francisco.

TO OUR READERS

WEISER BOOKS, an imprint of Red Wheel/Weiser, publishes books across the entire spectrum of occult and esoteric subjects. Our mission is to publish quality books that will make a difference in people's lives without advocating any one particular path or field of study. We value the integrity, originality, and depth of knowledge of our authors.

Our readers are our most important resource, and we appreciate your input, suggestions, and ideas about what you would like to see published. Please feel free to contact us to request our latest book catalog or to be added to our mailing list.

Red Wheel/Weiser, LLC
P.O. Box 612
York Beach, ME 03910-0612
www.redwheelweiser.com